Journal
of
The Rev. Godfrey Drehr
- 1819-1851 -

Transcribed by:
Brent H. Holcomb

Southern Historical Press, Inc.
Greenville, South Carolina

Copyright 1978 by:
The Rev. Silas Emmett Lucas, Jr.

All rights reserved. No part of this publication may be
reproduced, stored in a retrieval system or transmitted
in any form or by any means without the
prior permission of the publisher.

SOUTHERN HISTORICAL PRESS, INC.
PO BOX 1267
Greenville, SC   29601

ISBN #978-0-89308-060-8

Printed in the United States of America

To my pastor

THE REV. JOHN LLOYD SATTERWHITE III

who puts up with my wrong notes and complaints and still provides an excellent sermon every week.

INTRODUCTION

Godfrey Drehr was born 4 December 1789, the son of John and Ann Drehr. (See "Early Records of St. Michael's Lutheran Church, The South Carolina Magazine of Ancestral Research, Vol. IV, #4). He should not be confused with his uncle by the same name. Rev. Godfrey Drehr was licensed in 1810 and ordained in 1812, and served many churches, as can be seen by the contents of this volume. He died 18 July 1875, and is buried in St. Michael's Lutheran Church cemetery, near Irmo, S. C. (See A History of the Lutheran Church in South Carolina, for more information.). He was one of the most valuable Lutheran ministers in South Carolina.

This journal can be viewed on microfilm in the South Caroliniana Library, from which film this copy was transcribed. It begins in 1819 and ends in 1851. If journals before or after this period exist, they are not known to the writer. In many cases, the vital dates contained in this volume cannot be obtained elsewhere. Some deeds and probate records on persons mentioned in this journal can be found in Memorialized Records of Lexington District, by the writer, covering the period 1815-1825. The following are brief notes on some of the churches mentioned in the journal.

Bethlehem Church (Broad River) near Ballentine, S. C. on Highway 176, a church of the 1788 Corpus Evangelicum.

Bethlehem Church (Newberry) two miles west of Pomaria, off Highway 176, established 1813.

Hollow Creek Church--probably Salem or St. Pauls

Lybrands (Librands) Church or St. James--extinct by c. 1847

Mt. Calvary church near Johnston, S. C.

Nazareth Church Route 3, Lexington, S. C.

St. Jacob Church (Wateree Creek) in upper Richland County near the Newberry County line, about two miles off Highway 176(Corpus Evangelicum 1788)

St. John's Church about three miles east of Pomaria, off Highway 176, established c. 1754

St. Luke's church (Stony battery) near Prosperity, S. C., established c. 1829

St. Mark's Church (Edgefield) in present Saluda County

St. Michael's Church near Irmo, S. C. off Highway 60, established 1813

St. Paul's Church (Little Hollow Creek) near Gilbert, S. C., also known as Tawls or Ralls church, established c. 1803

St. Peter's (Meetze's) Church near Lexington, S. C. (Corpus Evangelicum 1788)

St. Peter's (Piney Woods) Church near Chapin, S. C. incorporated 1794

Salem (Hollow Creek) near Leesville, S. C. disbanded 1926, (Corpus Evangelicum 1788)

Sandy Run Church near Swansea, S. C.

Zion Church on Corley Mill Road, off Highway 378 between West Columbia and Lexington, (Corpus Evangelicum 1788)

Long's Church near Delmar and Leesville, extinct c. 1862

Brent H. Holcomb, G. R. S.
Columbia, S. C.
August 12, 1977

Page 1: A Journal commenced May 1819.
Sunday May 2. Preached at St. Peters.
Sunday May 9.   Do   at Wateree Creek.
   Do   Do 16   Do   at St. Michaels from 3 Cor.
Buried Daniel Coogle on the 17 of May.
Ascensions Day [Preached] at Lybrands Church.
Sunday 23 Preached at Bethlaham.
Saturday, Sunday 29, 30 Preached at St. Peters Church from
the 51 Psalm verse 4 and on Sunday from St. John 14:15 and
administered the Sacrament & received on adult[interlined]

June Sunday 6: Preached at the new church on broad river
from John 3.
Sunday 13 Preached in St. Johns from Luke 16, 19.
Sunday 20 P. in St. Michaels from Luke 14, 16 on Monday
24 [stricken]
Sunday 27. P. in Bethlaham from Luke 15.

July Sunday 4. P. in Lybrands church from the Gospel
Luke 6:36.
Buried Mathias Coogle on the 6.
on Saturday & Sunday 10 & 11 Brother Smoke & myself P.
at Sandy Run. He P. on Saturday from John 21, 17 & I P.
from Mark 8, 38. I P. on Sunday from St. John 21, 17 and
he P. from St. John 18. I find no falt in him. We then
administered the Sacrement.
Sunday 18. P. in St. Michaels from 1 Cor. 18 & Baptized
4 Children.
Sunday 25. P. at Bethlaham from 2 Thes. 1; 7, 8.
Sunday the 1 of August P. at Librands Church from the
Gospel Mat. 7: 15-21.

Page 2: Sunday August 8 P. at St. Peters Church from Isai 1:2[?]
Sunday 15 P. at St. Michaels from the Gospel Luke 18.9
& Baptised 2 white children.
Sunday 29 P. at St. Johns from Isaiah 1, 2, & & Baptised
one white child.
Sunday September 7. P. at Peters church from the Gospel
Luke 10: 25 and Baptised 2 white children.
Sunday 12th P. at Sandy Run Church from Mark 10.17. Baptised 2 white Children & recd Godfrey Kersh & his wife
into membership.
Sunday 19. P. at St. Michaels from the epistle Gal. 6.11-
18 and Baptised 4 black Children.
Tuesday 21. Married Jacob Harman to Elizabeth Wise &
Preached from Heb. 13.4.
Sunday 26. P. at Bethlaham Church Newbery from the Gospel
Luke 7.16 & Baptised one white child.
Sunday 30th Married William Taylor to Rebekah Corley.

Page 3: October 1819. Sunday 3rd P. at Librands Church from the
Epistle Eph. 4:1
Tuesday the 5th Married George Wise to Molly Roberts.
Thursday 7th. Married John Eiglebarger to Elizabeth Roof
and Baptised one white child.
Sunday 10th P. at Peters church from Heb. 12 and Baptised
one white child.
Sunday 17th P. at St. Michaels from the Epistle Ephes.
4.30.
Thursday 21. Married David Drehr to Rebekah Shular.
Sunday 24 P. at Bethlaham in Newberry from the Gospel
Mat 22. 1 and Baptised one white child.

Tuesday 26. Married William Wingard to Elender Burge.
Sunday 31. Preached at Bethleham on Broad river from the Gospel John 4. 46.
[November]
Sunday 7. P. at Peters Church from the Gospel Mat. 18.21.
Saturday Friend Smoke and myself, attended at Sandy Run I P. from Heb. 4.1 and Baptised one white child, and on Sunday we both Preached. I preached from the 43 Psalm verse 8 Confirmed 3 Adults, we then administered the Sacrament.
Sunday 21. P. at St. Michaels from 2 Cor. 5.20.
Sunday 28. P. at St. Johns from Rom. 13, 11 where Brother Shearer administered the sacrament to 11 Communicants.

Page 4: December 1819
Sunday 5th attended at Bethel Church where the Revd. Shearer & Francklow administered the Sacrament.
Thursday the 9th. Married Samuel Koon to Mary Ann Dupryee.
Sunday 12. Preached at Peters church from the Gospel Mat. 11. 2--and Baptised 2 white children.
Sunday 19. P. at the wateree creek Church from the Gospel St. John 1. 19.
On Saturday the 19. Buried West Coughmans child and preached from Rev. 14. 13.
On Christmas day Saturday 25 P. at St. Michaels from Mat. 1, 21 and on Sunday 26. Br. Metze and Rauch and myself administered the holy Sacrament. I baptised one white and two black children.

Page 5: January 1820
Saturday 1, or Circumcision of Christ. I preached at Bethlaham church on broad River.
Sunday the 2nd P. at Librands church from Titus 3, 4-7.
Thursday the 6 being Epiphany I P. at St. Michaels from Mat. 2.2 and Baptised Shulars child.
Sunday 9. P. at Peters Church from the Epistle Rom 12. 1-6.
Sunday 16 P. at St. Michaels from the Epistle Rom. 12.6 and married William See to the widow Boozer.
Sunday 23. I did not Preach owing to the rain.
Friday 28. P. a Funeral Sermon at Capt. Revises from 1 Cor. 15.22.
Sunday February 5th P. at the New Church at Librands from the Gospel Luke 8.4.
Sunday 13 P. at St. Peters from Psalm 19. 7, 8. and Baptised one white child.
Thursday 10. Married Philip Dubart to Polly Bernart.
Thursday 17th Married Jacob Nichols to Mary Dubart.
Sunday 20th. Married Mathias Coogler to Elizabeth Weed. I then went and preached at St. Michaels from the Gospel Mat. 4 & Baptised one Wt. c.

Page 6: February 1820.
Sunday 27. P. in Newberry from the Gospel Mat. 15. 21-28 and Baptised 5 white Children.
March 5. P. at Peters Church from the Gospel Luke 11. 14 and Baptised one white Child.
Sunday 12. P. at St. Johns Church from the Epistle Gal 4. 21 and Baptised 3 Children.
Sunday 19th P. at St. Michaels from the Gospel St. John 8.46--and Baptised 2 black Children.

Sunday 26th P. Bethleham Newbery John 15. 13 and Baptised
3 Children.
Good Friday P. at St. Michaels from 1 Cor. 5. 7,8.
Easter Sunday Br. Metze and myself P. I preached from
St. Luke 22. 19 and administered the Scarament.
Easter Monday. I preached at Bethlaham on Broad River
and Baptised one child.
Sunday 9 of April. Br. Shearer and myself Preached Beth-
leham Church in Newbery. I P. from Mat. 5.6. We admini-
stered the Sacrament, and Baptised one Child and Con-
firmed 2 Adults.
Thursday 13. Married Jacob Gramner to Nancy Dent.

Page 7: Sunday 16. Preached a Funeral Sermon from Heb. 4.9 on
the death of Fed. Keley's child named David Milder.
Saturday 22nd P. at Sandyrun from St. Luke 15. 18,19 and
on Sunday 23rd I preached from Mat 5.6 and Br. Smoke and
Myself administered the Sacrament.
Saturday 29th P. at Bethlehem church from Luke 15. 18,19
and on Sunday 30th P. from Mat 5.6 and administered the
Sacrament.
Sunday May the 7th P. at Peters Church from the Gospel St.
John 16 and Baptised 4 Children.
Thursday 11th being Ascensions day. P. at Bethlaham
Church from the Epistle Acts L. & Baptised 1 Child.
Sunday 15. P. at St. Michaels Church from Gal. 4.6.
Saturday the 20th Br. Metze & myself P. at St. Peters.
I P. from 1 John 1.9 and on Sunday the 21 being Whit-
sunday we Preached and administered the Sacrament. I
P. from the Gospel St. John 14.18 and baptised 2 Children.
On Monday 21 P. Librands Church from St. John 3.16 and
baptised one child.
Wednesday 23 P. the Funeral for David Boozers Child from
Mat. 25. 34.

Page 8: June 1820.
Sunday the 4 P. at St. Peters from Ga. 1,3.
Sunday the 11 attended the Sunday School for the first
time at st. Michaels Church with 16 Scholars, it being
a very rainy morning.
Monday 12. attended the Funeral of Henry Tarrer & Preached
from 1 Peter 1, 24, 25.
Sunday 18 P. at St. Michaels from the Gospel Luke 15.7 and
baptised 3 black children.
Thursday 22nd Married John Comalander to Margaret Nichols
and Conrod Shu___.[lar?] to Caty Gable.
Sunday 25. attended at Bethleham Newberry and Baptised 10
Children.
July. Sunday 2nd attended at St. Peters from 1 Peters
from 1 Peter 3.12.
Thursday 6th Married Jacob Harman to Barbara Stingley &
in the afternoon buried Polly Koon & Preached from Ec.
12.7.
Sunday 9. P. at St. Johns from Gal. 4.21-31.

Page 9: July 1820
Sunday 16th P. at St. Michaels from St. Luke 10.41-42--&
Baptised one Child.
Sunday 23. P. at Bethlaham, Newberry from the Epistle Rom
8, 12-17 & Baptised 6 Children.
Sunday 30 P. at Bethlehem B. River from the Gospel Luke
16.1-9.
August Tuesday 1, Buried Jacob Nichols & P. from Job. 14

1.2--
Sunday 20th P. at St. Michaels from Mat 23. 37 and in
the afternoon I P. the funeral Sermon for Mrs. Nichols
from Mat. 25.6.
September. Sunday 3rd P. at St. Peters from Luke 16, 29.
and in the afternoon I P. a funeral sermon for one of
George Loricks children & Baptised one.
Tuesday 5, P. a funeral sermon for one of Michael Crapses
Children from Mark 13. 35, 36.
Friday the 8, P a funeral sermon for one of Henry Hendrixs
Children from 1 Cor. 15.22.
Sunday 10. P. at Lybrands Church Ga. 6. 16 and Baptised
one child & on Monday buried George Freys Child.

Page 10: September 1820
Sunday 17th P. at St. Michaels from Luke 7.11.
Sunday 24 P. at Bethlehem in Newberry from Gal. 3, 23 and
Baptised 3 Children.
October Sunday 8th P. at Peters Church from Ma[sic]
13.44.
Tuesday 10th P. a Funeral Sermon for one of George Wises
children from Ps. 106.4.
Friday 14th P. funeral Sermon for Elizabeth Wise, daughter of the Widow Wise from Phil 1.21.
Sunday 22nd P. at Bethlehem church in New[berry] from the
Epistle Eph 6.10.
Monday 23, Buried Mrs. Coogle.
Tuesday 24. Buried Mrs. Bough & P. from Heb. 16.13.
Wednesday 25 Buried Harriet Hamiter & P. from Rev. 21.4.
Tuesday 31st Buried Mrs. George Stingley P. from Rev. 14.
13. Sunday 29 P. at Bethlehem Church on broad River from
the Gosple [sic] Mat. 18 and Baptised one child.

Page 11: November. Saturday 4, Buried James Smith & P. from
Lamentation 3. 22.
Sunday 5 P at Peters Church from the Gospel Mat. 22, 15-
22 & the same day P. a funeral Sermon for one of the
Miss Bones, from Luke 21.36.
Saturday 25 P. at Sandy run from Rom 13.11 and on Sunday
26 Br. Smoke & myself Preached & administered the Sacrament.
I P. from Ephe. 6, 10[?].
December Sunday 3 P at Peters Church from Rom. 13.11.
Sunday 10. Buried Mrs. Smoke & P. from Ps. 16.8.
Sunday 17. P. at Bethleham N. B. from the Gospel Mat.
11.
Sunday 24 P. at St. Michaels from the Epistle Phil 4.4
and Baptised 3 Children.
Monday 25, being Christmas day Br. Metze & Myself administered the Sacrament. I P. from St. John 1, 12 and Confirmed one Adult.
Sunday 31 Preached at Bethleham on Broad river from the
Epistle Ga. 1:1 and Baptised one Child.

Page 12: January 1821
Epiphany P. at St. James from
Sunday 7th Buried Jacob Liteses Wife and Baptised Two
children.
Sunday 14th P. at St. James from the Epistle Rom. 12.6
and Baptised Two children.
Sunday 21 P. at St. Michaels from the Gospel Mat 8,1.
February
Sunday 4th P at Peters from the Gospel Mat 13, 24-30 and

Baptised one Child.
Thursday 8 Married Henry Eleazer to Elizabeth Haltawanger.
Sunday 11 P at Bethleham on Broad River from the Epistle 1 John 3:1
Thursday 18th P. at St. Michaels Church from the Gospel Mat. 26.1--and Baptised one Child.
Sunday 25 P. at Newberry from the Gospel Luke 8:4 and Baptised 2 Children.

Page 13: March
Sunday 4, P. Sickness.
Sunday 11 P. at St. James from the Epistle 2 Cor. 6.1 and Baptised 1 Child.
Sunday 18. P. at St. Michaels from 2 Tim. 1:10. & Baptised 1 Child.
Sunday 25. P. at Newberry where Dr. Harris P. in my place. I Baptised 2 Children.
April
Sunday 1, P. at St. Peter from Rom 10.17.
Sunday 8. I did not Preach owing to the rain.
Sunday 15 P. at Newberry from the Gospel Mat. 27 and Baptised 2 Children.
Good Friday 20 P. at St. Michael with Br. Metze. I P. from St. John 19.5 and on Sunday we administered the Sacrament I P. from St. Luke 24, 34 and Baptised one White & two black Children on Easter Monday I P. in Edgefield from Luke 24, 34, & Baptised 5 Children.
Thursday 26. Married George Rackard to Mary Black [?].

Page 14: I did not Preach owing to the rain.
Sunday 6 of MAY P. in Mr. Metzes at St. Michaels.
Sunday 13 P. at St. James from the Gospel John 16.
Sunday 20 P. at St. Michaels from the Epistle James 1, and Baptised one Child, Reported to the Conference.
Sunday May 27. P. at Bethlaham in Newberry from the Epistle James 1, 22-27 & Baptised 3 Children. Tuesday 29 P. the Funeral for John Metz's Child from St. John 3.16.
Thursday 30. Ascension Day P. at Peters Church from the Epistle Acts 1.
JUNE Sunday 3rd, P. at Hollow Creek from James 1, 31 and Baptised 1 Child. Saturday 9 P. at Peters Church from 1 Cor 11, 28.29 and Confirmed 7 children & 3 adults [interlined "Whitsuntide"] and Sunday 10 P. from Epes. 4, 30 and aministered the Holy Sacrament & Baptised 1 Child.

Page 15: Whitsuntide Monday P. at Bethlem on Broad River from the Gospel st. John 3, from 16-21 & Baptised 1 Child.
Tuesday 12. Married John Bookman to Mary Magdalene Seastrunk.
Sunday 17 P. at St. Michaels from St. John 35.
Sunday 24 at Bethlahem in N. Berry from the Gospel Luke 16.
Thursday 28 P. the Funeral for one of George Grosses children.
July. Sunday 1. P. at Peters Church from the Gospel Luke 14. 16 Sunday 8 & Saturday 7. friend Metze & myself attended at St. James Church for the first time to administer the Sacrament on Saturday I preached from the 130 Ps 3, 4 & on Sunday from the 103 Ps. 13.

Sunday 15th P at St. Michaels from the Epistle Rom 8.18
Sunday 22 P. in Bethlehem in Newberry from Rom 5.1 &
Baptised 5 Children for Col. Cannon.
Sunday P at Zion Church from the Epistle Rom 6.23 &
Baptised one child.
Sunday 12 P. at St. James church from the Gospel Mat. 9. 15.

Page 16: August Sunday 19 P at St. Michaels Church from the Epistle 1 Cor 10.
Sunday 26 P. at Bethlehem in Newberry from St. John 1. 17 and Baptised one child.
Friday 31 P. the Funeral for John Lips from Rom 8.1.
September. Saturday 1 P. near Col. Lees from Rom 1. 16.
Sunday 2 P. at Peters Church from the Gospel Luke 18.9 & Baptised 2 Children.
Thursday 6 P at the funeral for Jacob Epting from 2 Peter 3.14.
Friday 7 P. at Zion Church inNewbery from Rom 8.1 & Baptised 2 Children & in the night Married Alexander Stewert to Mrs. Mayer.
Saturday 8 P at St. Johns church from Ro. 1,16 & Baptised 1 Child.
Sunday 9 P at wateree creek Church from Gal. 3.6 & Baptised 1 Child.
Monday 10 P the Funeral for one of Col. Countzes Children from Luke 21. 36.
Wednesday 12 Buried one of Counts children from Mat. 25. 46.

Page 17: Sunday 16 P at St. James Church from the Epistle Gal. 3:16.
Thursday 20 P. the Funeral for one of George Eiglebargrs Children from Luke 18.17.
Saturday 22 P. near Col. Lees from Mat. 9. 13.
Sunday 23 P. at Capt. Longs Church from Rom 10.4.
Sunday 30 P. at Bethlehem on Broad River from the Epistle Ga. 6.11.
OCTOBER Monday 1. P. the Funeral for Jacob Kleckleys Wife from 2 Peter 3. 14.
Sunday 7 P. at Peters Church.
Sunday 14 P at St. James.
Sunday 21 P. at St. Michaels & Baptised one child.
Sunday 28 P. at Bethlehem church in Newbery where Br. Moser & myself administered the Sacrament.
November. Sunday the 4. P. near John Wise from Mat. 25, 46.
Sunday 11 P. at St. Peters from the Gospel St. John 4, 46 & Baptised 2 Children.
Sunday 18 P at St. Michaels church from the Gospel Mat. 18.21.

Page 18: November Sunday 25. P. at Zion in Newberry with Br. Moser where we administered the Sacrament. I P. from John 6. 35.
Tuesday 27 Married Jacob Bickely to Jemima Smith.
December Sunday 2 P. at Peters from John 6. 35.
Sunday 16th P. at Bethlehem in Newberry from the Epistle 1 Cor 4.1.
Thursday 20th Married Jacob Nunemaker to Sharlet Younginer.
Sunday 23 P. at St. Michaels Church from 2 Cor 5.20 &

Baptised one child.
Tuesday being Christmas day I administered the Sacrament,
Read from Gospel Luke 2. 10.11 & Baptised 2 Children.
Wednesday 26 P. in Zion Church from 1 Tim. 1. 15.
Sunday 30 P. at Bethlehem on Broad river from the Gospel
Mat. 1. 21.

Page 19: January 1822.
Tuesday 1. P. at Peters Church from the Gospel Luke 2.
15-21 & Baptised 2 Children.
Thursday 3 Married Jacob Kleckley to Fannie Hamiter.
Sunday 6 P. at Caughmans Church from the Gospel Mat. 2.
Sunday 13 P at St. James from the Epistle Rom. 12. 1.
Baptised 2 children.
Sunday 20 P. at St. Michaels from Rom 6.14.
Tuesday 22 Married Thomas L. Veale to Harriet Rieves.
Sunday 3 February P. at Peters Church from the Gospel.
Sunday 10. P. at St. James from the Gospel & Baptised
2 children.
Thursday 14 Married David Hamiter to Harriet Kleckley.
Sunday 24 P. at St. John's Church from 2 Cor. 12.
March 3 Sunday P. at Peters Church from the Epistle
1 Thess 4.1.

Page 20: March 1822
Sunday 10. Rain.
Thursday 14 married John Rall to Elizabeth Austen and
Baptised 1 Child.
Sunday 17. P. at St. Michaels from Luke 18.21, 22.
Sunday 24 P. at St. Peters from the Gospel John 8. 46 &
Baptised 2 Children.
Sunday 31 P at Bethlehem on Broad River from the Epistle
Phil. 2.5.
Good Friday April 5 I P. at Bethlehem on broad river from
Isa. 53.6.
Saturday 6 friend Metze & myself P. at St. Michaels where
I confirmed 16 Persons & then P. from Heb. 10.23 & Baptised 2 Children and on Easter Sunday I P. from 1 Cor.
15. 20-22 and administered the Sacrament to upwards of
one hundred com. & Baptised 2 black children.
Sunday 14 P. at St. James's church from the Gospel John
20:19.
Sunday 21 P. at St. Michaels from 1 Peter 12.19 & Baptised 1 Child.
Thursday 25 P. the funeral for Jacob Harmans Child
from Luke 18.16

Page 21: Sunday 28 P. at St. Mathews church from Heb. 10.23 &
Baptised 1 Child.
May Sunday 5th P. the funeral sermon for John Stingley
from Heb. 11. 16.
Sunday 12 P. near John Wises from Mat. 7.13.14 Baptised
1 white & 1 black child.
Thursday 16 being Ascension day P. at St. James from the
Epistle Acts 1.
Sunday 19 P. at St. Michaels from the Epistle 1 Peter
4. 7,8. and Baptised 1 white & 1 black child.
      Returned to Synod
Sunday June 17th P. at Bethlehem Newberry from St. John
3. 16-21.
Sunday 23 P. at Sandy run from Rom. 8.1.
Sunday 30th P. at Bethlehem on broad river from the

Epistle Rom 8. 18-23 Baptised 2 Children.
Sunday July 7 P. at Peters Church from the Epistle 1
Peter 3.8.15 and Baptised 1 Child.
Thursday 11th Married John Frey to Christena Hendrix.

Page 22: Sunday 14 P. at St. James from Rom 6. 3-11.
Sunday 21 P. at St. Michael from Rom 6. 23.
Sunday 28 P. at Bethlehem church in Newbery from Rom.
8. 14. Baptised 3 children.
Thursday August 1 Married Jacob Stingly to Barbara
Derick.
August 4 P. in edgefield from the Gospel Luke 16. 1-9.
Baptised 3 children.
Sunday 11th P. at John Wises from Gospel Luke 19.41.
Sunday 18 P. at St. Michaels from the Gospel Luke 18.19.
Sunday 25 P. at Amelia from Rom 8.14.
Setpember Sunday 1 P. at St. Peters from the Epistle
Ga. 3.16 and Baptised 1 Child.
Sunday 8 P. at St. James from the Epistle Ga. 5.16.
Tuesday 10 Buried one of John Bouknights children named
Christenah P. from Mat. 24.44.
Sunday 15th P. at St. Michaels Church from the Epistle
Gal. 6. 11.
Sunday 22 P. at John Wises from Mat 5.20.
Sunday 29 P. at Bethlehem Church from the Gospel Luke
14.7 & Baptised 2 Children.
October Sunday 6th P. at Peters church from the 4# of
Rom. Verse 8.
Sunday 13th P. at St. James

Page 23: church from the Epistle Ephes 4. 23.
Wednesday 2 P. the funeral for Gabriel Hoylers Wife and
baptised his Child from Rom 6. 23.
Friday the 4 of October P. the Funeral for Srums [?]
child from 1 Cor 15.22.
Saturday 19 P. the funeral for Bookmans child from Rom.
6. 23.
Sunday 20 P at St. Michaels from the Gospel Mat 22. 1-13
& Baptised 1 Child.
Tuesday 22 Married Mathias Wessinger to Leah Carline
Hornsby.
Sunday 27th Rain day.
Novr Sunday 3 P. at St. Peters from the Gospel Mat. 23-35
& Baptised one Child.
Tuesday 5 Married Christian Wessinger to Caty Comalander.
Saturday & Sunday the 9.10 the Rev. Metze & myself P. at
St. James I P. from St. John 6. 63 & on Sunday I P. from
1 John 3.1. we then administered the Lord Supper.
Saturday & Sunday 16 & 17 Rauch & myself P. at Bethle-
hem in Newberry. I P. from St. John 6. 63 on Sunday I P.
from 1 John 3.1. We then administered the Sacrament.
Sunday 24 P. at St. Michaels from the Epistle 1 Thes
4. 13-18 Baptised 2 Children.

Page 24: December Sunday 1 P at Peters from 2 Peter 3. 11 &
Baptised 1 Child.
Sunday 8. P at Piney Woods Church from Ephes. 5,8, from
the church I went to Wiggers & Married Henry Hart to
Susan Gartman.
Sunday 15 P. at Zion Church from 1 John 3.1.
Sunday 22 P. at St. James's Church from Gal. 4, 4,5 &
Baptised 1 Child.

Tuesday & Wednesday 24.25 being Christmas Metze, Rauch, Hersher & myself attended at St. Michaels and administered the Sacrament and confirmed 1 Adult.
Sunday after Christmas I P. at Bethlehem on broad river from Ga. 4,4.
1823 January 5. Sunday P at Peters Church from 1 Peter 4 17.18. Baptised 1 Child.
Sunday 12 P. at James Church, where the Revd. Shoneback attended & preached in my place.
Sunday 19 P. at Michaels Church from Mat 6. 33.
Sunday 26th P. in Zion Church. Buried Christinah Tarrer.

Page 25: from 1 Cor 1, 21
Sunday 2nd of February P. in Peters C. from Heb. 2.3.
Wednesday 5 a day appointed by the Governor. P. at Peters C. from Prov. 14.34 & Baptised 1 Child.
Sunday 9. Snowed.
Sunday 16 P. at St. Michaels from the Epistle 2 cor 6.2.
Sunday 23 P. at Zion Church from Rom. 1. 16. Baptised 3 Children.
Sunday 2 of March 1823.
P. at Hollow Creek from 2 Cor 6.2. baptised one child.
Sunday 9 P. at Jameses C. from Ephes. 2.1. Baptised 2 children.
Sunday 16 P.at St. Michaels from the Epistle Heb. 9.11-15 and Baptised 2 children.
Sunday 24 P at Bethlehem on broad river from 2 Cor 5.15 and baptised one child.
Sunday 30 Easter friend Metze & myself P and administered the Sacrament at St. Michaels I P. from 1 Peter 1.3.

Page 26: From Easter untill a few days before Whitsuntide I spent in visiting in North Carolina 1823. Tuesday the 8th of April we started to Father Millers and returned from N. C. on the 12 of May. On Saturday & Sunday the 17 & 18 of May being Whitsun Br. Metze & myself attended at Peters Church I P. from St. James 4.8 and Br. Metze P. from John 3.1. Sunday I P. from St. John 3.5 I then administered the holy Sacrament.
Trinity Sunday 25 P. in Zion Church from the Gospel John 3.1-15.
Sunday 1 of June, I P in Peters church from the Gospel Luke 16, 19-31, and baptised one child.
Sunday the 8th of June, I P. in St. James Church from Mat 11, 28 and baptised one child.
Sunday the 15th of June P at St. Michaels from the Epistle 1 Peter 5.5.
Sunday 22 in Zion Church where Br. Hersher P. in my place.
Sunday 29 P in Bethlehem church on broad river from the Epistle 1 Peter 3.8 & Baptised 2 Children.
Monday 30 P the Funeral for David Metze from 1 Thes 5.2 & Br. Hersher exhorted in english & German.
Sunday 6th of July P. in hollow creek Church

Page 27: from Heb. 2.3 & Baptised one child.
Sunday 13 P. in Peters church from the epistle Rom 6.19.
Sunday 20th P. in St. Michaels from the Epistle Rom 8. 12.
Thursday 24 Married Reuben Harman to Luesia Rouch.
Sunday 27 P in St. Pauls church on hollow creek where the Rev. Hersher attended with me.
August Sunday 10th P. in Peters Church from Rom 8. 3,4.

Sunday 17th P. in St. Michaels Church from Gal. 2.20 & Baptised one child.
Sunday 24 P. in Bethlehem church on broad river from Ephes. 2.8.
Wednesday 27 P the Funeral for Henry Highs son John from Col. 3.3,4.
Novr 6 Married Saml Kerich to Susannah Younginger.
Saturday & Sunday the 15 & 16 We Preached & administered the Sacrament in St. Michaels Church.

March 1824

Sunday 7 P in Peters Church but before preaching I married Scott to Rebekah Metzd, after the mariage we went to the Church & I preachd from 2 Cor 6 & Baptised one child.
Sunday 14th The Rev. Rudy and myself preached and administered the Sacrament in Bethlehem Church on Broad River.

Page 28: Thursday 18. Married Martin Coughman to Barbara Harman.
Sunday 21 P in St. Michaels from The strong man armed & Baptised 1 Child.
Sunday 28 P again in St. Michaels in Rev. Metzes place.
Sunday the 4th of April P in St. Johns Church with the Rev. Hersher & Rauch & Ordained Moser.
Sunday 11th P. in St. Peters from John 12.24 & Baptised 1 Child.
Good Friday 16 Rev. Metze & myself P. in St. Michaels I P. from St. John 1.29.
On Easter Sunday again I P. from Col. 3.1 & administered the Sacrament & Baptised 1 Child.
Sunday 25 P. in Nazareth in the Sandhills from St. John 1.29.
Sunday the 2 of May P. in St. Michaels from
Sunday 8 & 9 in Zions Church with the Rev. Franklow. I P. from Luke 13.5 & on Sunday from Heb. 4.16 we then administered the Sacrament.
Sunday 16 P in Peters Church from
Sunday 23rd P. in Bethlehem C. on Broad river.
Sunday 30th P. in St. James Church from 1 Peter 4.7-__.
On Thursday 20th we ordained the Rev. Mr. Mealy.

Page 29: June. Sunday 5 & 6 being Whitsunday P. in Peters Church on Saturday I P. from Mark 1.15 & confirmed 2 Adults & on Sunday I P from Revelation 22,17. The Rev. Bealem [?] P. from Rom. 6. 21-23. I then administered the Sacrament to about 60 persons.
Sunday 13. Father Metze & myself P. in Nazareth Church in the Sand hills from 1 John 3 1.2. and administered the Sacrament .
Sunday 20 P in St. Michaels Church from 1 John 3.4
Sunday 27th P. in Zion Church from Rom 4.3.
Here I commenced preaching for one year, one Sermon in each month.
Sunday the 4th of July 1824 P. in Peters Church from the Gospel Luke 15:1 Baptised 2 Children.
Sunday 11 P. in the sandhills in Nazareth Church from the Epistle Rom 8.18
Sunday 18 P. in Zion Church from the Epistle 1 Peter 3.8, and Baptised 3 Children.
Sunday 25 P. in Bethlehem Church on Broad River from the Gospel Mat. 5.20.

August Sunday 1 P. in Zion Church from the Epistle Rom 6.19
Sunday 15 P. in St. Michaels Church from the Gospel St. Luke 16:1-9 and Baptised 2 Children.

Page 30: Sunday 22 P. in Bethlehem Church on Broad River from Heb. 4.1-2.
Sanday 29 P. in St. James Church from the Epistle 1 Cor 15.
Sunday 5 of September P. in Peters Church from Heb. 4. 1-2 and Baptised 2 Children.
Sunday 12 Rain.
Sunday 19 P in St. Michaels from Luke 10.25 Baptised one child.
Sunday 3rd of October. P. in Peters Church from St. John 3.7 and Baptised one child.
Thursday 7 P. a funeral sermon for Kerick wife from 1 Cor. 7.29.
Saturday & Sunday the 9 & 10 P. in Sandy run from St. John 3.7 & Baptised 2 Children & Confirmed 2 Adults. On Sunday I P. from Luke 10.25 and administered the Sacrament.
Sunday 17th P in St. Michaels from 1 Cor 6.19-20 and Baptised 2 Children.
Sunday 24 P in Bethlehem from Prov. 14.32.
Sunday 31 P in St. James Church from the gospel Mat. 22.1
Tuesday the 2nd of November Married Doctr. Irby to Mary Eiglebarger and on Thursday the 4 Married David Coogle to Milly Wingard.
Sunday the 7th P. in Peters Church from Rom 1.16.
Tuesday 9 P a Funeral for one of Henry Metz Children from Mat 24.44.

Page 31: A Journal recommenced [?] after our Synod in November 1824.
On Friday the 26 of November I baptised Jacob Huffmans child, and on Saturday the 27 I preached its Funeral Sermon from Rev. 14,13.
Sunday 28 P in St. Michaels from Rom. 10.15.
Thursday 2 of December, I married Daniel Gartman to Elizabeth Dent recd $4.
Saturday 4. Preached a Funeral for one of John Corleys sons from Rev. 14.13.
Sunday 5 P in Peters church from the Gospel Luke 21.36 and Baptised 2 children.
Sunday the 12th P. in Zion Church from the Gospel Mat. 11 2-10.
Thursday 16 Married Adam Roberts to Tempy Rauch recd $2.
Sunday the 19 Prevented on account of the river, being _?_.
Christmas, Saturday 25 P. from 2 Chron. 7.4,5 and Dedicated Salem Church on Hollow Creek.
Sunday 26 P in St. Michaels Church from Luke 2.10 where Father Metze & the Rev. Belen Preached and after preaching we administered the Sacrament.

Page 32: January 1825.
Sunday the 2 of January P in Peters Church from Jeremiah 28.16. This year thou shalt die. $11.50
Thursday the 6 of January P in St. Jameses Church from the Gospel St. Mat. 2.2.
Sunday the 9th P. in Zion Church from the Epistle Rom. 12.1. The Rev. Houk also attended.
Sunday the 16th P. in St. Michaels c. from 1 Cor. 3.11.

and Baptised 4 Children.
Thursday the 20 Married Capt. Andrew Derrick to Caty Kleckly. $1.00.
Sunday 23. Snow _____ went off on the 26.
Thursday 27. Married George White to Catharine Metze $1. and also Gabriel Hoyler to Abigal Gartman $2.
Sunday 30 P in St. James from Rom 10.10. $4.50
Sunday 6 P. in Peters C. from the gospel Luke 8.8. and Baptised 2 Children $1.50.
February Sunday 13 P in Zion from the Epistle 1 Cor. 13.
Sunday 20 P in St. Michaels from the Gospel Mat. 4.

Page 33: Thursday 24 Married John Wingard to Sarah Effler. $1.00
Saturday 26 P. the Funeral for Lewis Stacks child from Rev. 14.13 and Baptised one child and recd $2 from John Stack.
Sunday 27 P. in Bethlehem church on broad river from
Sunday 6th of March P. in Peters Church from Prov. 22.6 and baptised one child.
Sunday 13th P. in Zion Church from Ephes 6.1-4 and baptised one child.
Sunday 20 P in St. Michael Church from Prov. 4.1 and in the afternoon, Buried old Mrs. Shuler & P from St. John s.28.29 $1
Sunday 27 Father Metze & myself P in Nazareth church. I preached from Rom 8.32 and administered the Sacrament to 20 Communicants and recd $3.62½ Cents.
Good friday 1 of April Confirmed in St. Michaels Church 23 persons & recd $12.1 [amt. unclear]
Sunday the 3d Easter Sunday Father Metze & myself P in St. Michaels I P from Mat 28.6 and administered the Sacrament to 120 Comts & bap 1 child $1.

Page 34: Easter Monday the 4 of April P. in Zion Church from St. Luke 24.13-35 & baptised 1 child.
Sunday 10th P. in Bethlehem church in Newberry from the Gospel St. John 20.19-31 and Baptised 3 children $2.50.
Saturday 23 of April Father Franklow & myself P in Zion Church from 1 John 1:8.9 and Baptised one child.
Sunday 24 I P. from the Gospel John 16.16-23 and Father Franklow and myself administered the Sacrament to about 80 Comt and Baptised one child.
Sunday 8 P. in Bethlehem on Broad River from Prov. 22.6 and Baptised 2 children. in the after noon, preached the funeral for old Mought from 1 Cor 15.55.
Sunday 15th P in Zion church from the Epistle 1 Peter 4. 7-11 and Baptised 2 Children.

Page 35: Saturday 21 of May Father Metze & myself P. in Peters Church from Mat 5.4 Confirmed 12 young persons.
Whit Sunday 22. I preached from Rom 8.14 and administered the holy Sacrament to 90 persons. Baptised 3 Children.
Sunday 29 P in St. James Church from the Gospel st. John 3.1-15.
Sunday the 5th of June P. in Peters Church from the Gospel Luke 16.19-31.
Sunday 12 P in Nazareth church from the gospel Luke 14. 16-24 and Baptised 1 child.
Monday the 13 P the Funeral for one of Adam Metzes children from Heb. 2.3.

Sunday 19th P in St. Michaels from the Gospel Luke 15. 1-10.
Tuesday 21 Married John Thompson to Eve Gable $3.
Sunday 26 P in Zion Church from the Epistle Rom 8.18-23
Comment preachig for one year $17.25
Sunday 3 of July P in Peters Church from the gospel Luke 5.1-11.

Page 36: Sunday the 10th of July I Preached in Bethlehem Church on broad river from the Gospel Mat 5.20.
Sunday 17 P in St. Michaels from St. John 14.6 and Baptised 2 Children.
Sunday 24 P in Zion from the Gospel Mat 7.15-23 & Baptised 1 child.
Sunday the 31st P in St. Jameses church from the Gospel Luke 16 1-9.
Sunday the 7th of August P in the Piney Woods or Longs Church from St. John 14 C. and on Monday the 8 P at the schoolhouse below Clouds creek from Rom 5.1, and Baptised 5 Children and on Tuesday P in the Academy from Acts 16 30.31 and on Wednesday the 10 P in Salem above little Saluda from St. John 3.7.
Sunday the 14 P in Peters Church from the Gospel St. Luke 18.9 and Baptised 1 child.
Sunday the 21 an excessive rain.
Thursday the 25 Married Christian Wingard to Anna Catharine Nichols & recd $1.
Saturday the 27 P the Funeral for Barnet Hoyler from Heb. 9. 27 recd $1.
Sunday 28 P in Zion Church from the

Page 37: Gospel Luke 10.25-37 and in the after noon preached the Funeral sermon from 1 Peter 4.7 for John Weed.
Sunday the 4 of September P in Peters Church from the Gospel Luke 17.11-19.
Sunday the 11 P in Nazareth C. from the Epistle Gal. 6. 1-15 and Jacob Wingard Exhorted.
Tuesday 13 P the Funeral for one of John Weeds children from 2 Cor. 5.10.
Wednesday the 14 P a Funeral sermon for one of John Dericks Children from 2 Cor. 5.10.
Saturday the 17. P. in lower Hollowcreek Church from Heb. 2.3.
Sunday 18 P in Longs Church from Luke 10.25-37 and in the afternoon Preached the funeral for John Derick from Mat. 24.44 $2.
Thursday 22nd P the funeral for one of Jacob Jacksons children from Mat 24.44
Sunday the 25 P the funeral for one of George Wises Junr children from Rev. 14.13. $1.
Saturday October 1 P in St. Pauls Church from 1 Tim 1.15.
Sunday the Second P in Longs Church from Rom 10.4 & Baptised 1 child & in the afternoon P in Salem Church from Mat 16.26.
Sunday the 9 P in Bethlehem Church from Mat 16.26 Baptised 1 child and recd $9.

Page 38: October. Thursday the 13th Married Saml Metz to Mary Metz recd $1 and in the afternoon Married Jacob Stack to Rebecca Weed recd $1.
Sunday the 16 P in St. Michaels Church from 2 Tim. 3.15 and Baptised 3 children.

Sunday 23 P in Zion Church from the Gospel St. John 4. 47 and Baptised 1 child.
Thursday 27 Married Jesse Dreher to Elizabeth Shuler and on Friday the 28 Preached the Funeral for Jacob Metzes Wife from Heb 4.9.
Sunday the 30 P in St. Jameses church from
Monday 31 P the Funeral for one of Jacob Dericks Children, from Mat. 25.13 $1.
Friday the 4 of November P the funeral for one of Mrs. Weads children from Rom 5.18.
Sunday the 6 P in Peters Church from Rom. 5.18. Baptised 2 children.
Saturday the 12 P in St. Pauls church from 1 Cor. 1.21 and Sunday the 13 P in Longs Church from Rom 1.16 and in the afternoon P in Salem church from Rom 10.1.
Sunday the 20 P in St. Michaels Church from 1Cor 15.1.2.

Page 39: Sunday the 27 of November attended the Synod
Sunday the 4 of December P in Peters Church from Mat 6. 9-13.
Thursday the 1 of December Married Henry Bouknight to the Widow Bookman   recd $1.
Thursday the 8 Married David Hamiter to Mariah Beaty recd $3 and in the evening married George Gartman to Miss See recd $2.
Sunday morning the 11 of Decr Married Ezekiel Salser to Elisa Bezoon recd $2 and in the afternoon preached the funeral for Mrs. Haltawanger, from Psalm 48.14 $2.
Sunday the 18 P in Zion Church from the Epistle Phil.
Saturday the 24 Father Metze & Myself P preparatory to the Sacrament. I preached from Prov. 16.1 & Baptised 2 Children.
Christmas Sunday 25 P from Mat 1.21 and Father Metze & Myself administered the Sacrament to 120 Comts. and on Monday P in Bethlehem Church from Titus 2.14 & Baptised 1 Child.
        The whole amount of 1825 $125.

Page 40: January 1826
Sunday the 1 P in Peters Church from Luke the 13. 7.8.9 and Baptised 3 children. recd $21.20 $5.50
Sunday the 8 P in Sandyrun church from Titus 2.14 and on Thursday 12 P the funeral for George Drehers Wife from Rom 6.23.
Sunday the 15 P in Longs church from Titus 2.14.
Sunday the 22 P in Zion Church from the Gospel Mat. 20 1-16 and Baptised 2 children.
Thursday the 6 of January P in St. Michaels Church from Luke 2.32 Recd $15. 8.50 $23.50
Sunday 29 P in Bethlehem church bd r. the Rev. Wessels attended and preached.
February Thursday the 2 Married George Harman to Barbara Drehr $1
Sunday the 5 P in Peters church from the Epistle 1 Cor 13 and in the afternoon preached the funeral for George Roberts child from Rev. 14.15.
Saturday 11 P the funeral from 1 Cor 15.55 for George Roberts wife   Recd $1

Page 41: February 1826
Sunday 12 attended with the Rev. Wessels in Longs church recd $25.

Sunday the 19 P in St. Michaels from the Epistle 1 Thes 4.1 Baptised 1 child.
Sunday the 26 P in Zion Church from the Epis. Ephes 5.1 & Baptised 1 child.
March Saturday the 4 P the funeral for Lewis Stacks child & Baptised 1 child.
Sunday the 5th P in Peters Church from 1 Peter 4.1 and Baptised 1 child and on Thursday the 8 Married Wilm Gartman to Rebekah Crate recd $1.
Sunday 12 P in St. Michaels from the Epistle Heb. 9.
Sunday the 19 P in Zion Church from Phil 2.5.
Thursday 23 P in Zion Church from 2 Cor 13.5 and Baptised one child.
Friday 24 being Good Friday P in Zion from John 19.5 and administered the Sacrament to about 64 or 65 persons.
Saturday 25 P in Peters Church from Mark 1.15 & Easter Sunday Father Metz & myself P I Preachd from St. John 19.25 & we administered the Sacrament to 61 Comts.
Monday P. in Bethlehem Church B river

Page 42: April 1826
Wednesday 5 P the funeral for John Earharts daughter from Heb. 23.
Saturday the 8 P in Sandy run Church from St. Mark 1.15 & on Sunday I preached from the 116 Ps. and administered the Sacrament to about 40 Comt & Confirmed 2 adults. and Baptised 2 Children.
Tuesday 11 Married John Grigorey to Nancy Roof $2.00.
Sunday 16 P in St. Michaels Church from the Gospel John 16.16-23 & Baptised 3 children.
Sunday 23 P in Zion Church from the Gospel St. John 16 5-15 & Baptised 1 child.
Thursday 27 P the Funeral for Mrs. Huffman from Job 7. 9.10. $2.00
Friday 28 P in Zion from Mat 6.10
Sunday 30 P in Nazareth Church from 116 Psalm verse the 12.13.14 & administered the Sacrament to 15 Communicants and Baptised 2 children $2.50.

Page 43: May 1826
Sunday 7 P in St. Peters Church from St. John 3.18 and Baptised 1 child
Saturday the 18 P in St. Michaels from 1 Cor 11.28 & on Sunday 14 being Whitsunday Father Metze & myself P & administered the Sacrament I preached from Ephes 1.13 about 90 Communicants Baptised one child for which I recd $2 & I also recd from the Congregation $8.50.
Wednesday 17 P the funeral for Caty Rouch from Mat 24.42 recd $1.
Thursday 18 Married Jesse McCarty to Anna Weed recd $1
Sunday 21 P in Bethlehem church from the Gospel St. John 3.7.
Sunday 28 P in Zion from the Gospel Luke 16.19 & Baptised 3 children
Monday 29 P in St. Michaels from Levt. 26.4 in consequence of the dry weather.

Page 44: June 1826
Sunday 4 P in Peters Church from the Gospel Luke 14.15-24 & Baptised one child.
Thursday 8 P the funeral for John Freys Wife from Thessalonians 5.3 & Baptised 1 child.

Sunday 11 P in Nazareth Church from the Gospel Luke 15.
1-11.
Sunday June 18 P in St. Michaels Church from Luke 19.10
Friday 16 P. a thanks giving Sermon in Zion Church from
Acts. 14.17.
Sunday 17 P in Zion from Gal 6.14. Baptised one child.
$21.75
July Saturday 1 friend Smoke & Myself preached for the
first time in the new church in Amelia. I preached from
Luke 19.10.
On Sunday 2 I dedicated the Church (St. Mathews) &
preached from 2 Chrol. 7.5 & Smoke from Rev. 7.14. We
then administered the Sacrament.
Sunday 9 P in Bethlehem from the Epistle Rom 6.19-23.
$3.25

Page 45: Sunday 16 P in St. Michaels from the Epistle Rom. 8.
12-17.
Friday 21 P the funeral sermon for John Shulers wife from
Ps. 31.5
Sunday 23 P in Zion from the Gospel Luke 16.1-9
Sunday 30 P in Bethlehem from Luke 19. 41-48.
August 1826
Sunday 6 P in St. Peters from the Gospel Luke 18.9-14
Baptised one child.
Friday 4 P the funeral for one of Jacob Huffamers child-
ren from Rev. 7.14
Sunday evening 13 Married Polly Hoyler to John Bright.$2.
Sunday 20 P in St. Michaels Church from the Gospel Luke
10.23-37 & Baptised one child.
Friday 25 P the funeral for old Mrs. Earhart from St.
John 5.25 $1.
Sunday 27. P in Zion Church from Rom 10.1 Baptised one
child.

Page 46: September 1826
Sunday 3 P in Bethlehem from the Gospel Mat. 6.24-34.
Wednesday the 6 P the funeral for Rev. Rauchs daughter
from Mat 18.3.
Sunday 10 P in Peter Church from the epistle Ephes 3.
13-21
Sunday the 17 P in St. Michaels Church from Rom 10.1
and Baptised one Child.
Sunday 24 P in Zion Church from the Gospel Mat. 22.34-46.
October Sunday 1 P in Peter church from the Gospel Mat.
9.1-8.
Thursday 12 P the funeral for one of George Likes daughter
from Heb. 9.27.
Sunday 15 P. in St. Michaels church from the
Thursday 19 I visited Michael Leapharts Wife & gave her
the Sacrament.
Sunday morning the 22 administered the Sacrament to Mrs.
Mathias & at 10 oclock preached in Zion Church from the
Gospel Mat. 18.23-35 & in the afternoon 3 oclock P the
funeral for Jacob Harmans [?] child from Luke 10.42 & at
4 oclock P the funeral for Saml Swigard.

[no explanation for the gap here]

Page 47: December 1827
Sunday the 2 of December P in Peters Church from the
Epistle Rom 13.11-14

Wednesday 5 P the Funeral for Gaminer from 2 Cor 5.1
Sunday the 9 P at Sandy run Church from 2 Cor 13.5-11.
Sunday 16 P at St. Michaels from Heb. 2.3. & Baptised
2 Children.
Thursday night 20 Married Jesse Owens to Miss Effler.
Sunday 23 P at Zions Church from Luke 2.10 & Baptised
2 Children.
Monday 24 Buried Jacob Kellys child & P from 2 Cor 5.10
Tuesday 25 Christmas Day Father Meetze & myself P. at St.
Michaels Church from 1 Tim 1-15 & in the afternoon I
buried John Bouknights Wife & P from Heb. 11.16.
Wednesday the 26. Father Meetze, Wingard & myself met
at St. Michaels, Meetze & Wingard P & we then administered the Sacrament to 49 Communicants I Baptised one
Child.

Page 48: Sunday 30 P at Bethlehem B. R. from Gal. 4.1-7 & Baptised Mrs. Bookman and her Child.
Monday 31. I Baptised Capt. Huffmans child.
Tuesday January 1, 1828. P at Nazareth Ch. from Gal.
6.15.
Sunday 13 I P at St. Mathews Church Orangeburg from
Gal. 4.1-7 on my return from Charleston.
Sunday 20 P at St. Michaels from Rom 12.2 and Baptised
one child.
February Sunday 3 P at St. Peters from the Gospel Mat
20.1-16 Baptised one child   recd $14.25.
Sunday 10 P at Bethlehem from the Gospel Luke 8 4-15
Recd $10.10
Sunday 17 P at St. Michaels Church from the Epistle
1 Cor 13. Baptised 2 Children.
Sunday 24 Prevented in consequence of high water.

Page 49: March Sunday 2 P at St. Peters from the Epistle 1 Thes.
4.1-7 & Baptised 1 Child.
Sunday 9 P at Nazareth from the Epistle Epes 5.1-13
Baptised 3 Children.
Sunday 16 P at St. Michaels Church from Col. 2. 6.7. recd
$20 and on Friday 21 Baptised Stacks child.
Sunday 23 P at Zion Church from the Epis Heb. 9.13-14 &
Baptised one child.
Sunday 30 the Rev. John Schwartz P for me at Bethlehem
Church Broad River.
Thursday 3rd of April at St. Michaels Church from the
116 Psalm & 12-14 verse & on Good Friday I Preached
from St. John 12.32 & Father Metze, Rauch & myself administered the Sacrament to about 50 Communicants & Baptised
one Child.
Saturday the 5 Wingard & myself P at Zion Church I
preached from St. Luke 15.18 & on Easter Sunday. Father
Meetze & Wingard P we then administered the Sacrament
to about 100 Communicants & I Baptised 3 children.
Saturday the 12 P the funeral for Lewis Stacks child
from Mat 25.46.

Page 50: Sunday 13 P at Peters Church from the Gospel St. John
20.19-31 & Baptised 2 Children.
Thursday 17 P the Funeral for old Mrs. Caughman from Heb.
4.9
Sunday 20 P at St. Michael from   & Baptised 2 Children.
Sunday 27 P at Peters Church from the Gospel St. John 16.
16-23 & Baptised 2 Children.
Sunday the 4 of May Preached in the Rev. Bachmans Church

Charleston from Rom. 1.16.
Sunday 11 P at Nazareth Church from St. Luke 15.18.19 & Baptised 3 Children.
Ascensions day P at Bethleham from Ephes 4.8 & Baptised 1 child.
Sunday 18 P at St. Michaels from the Epistle 1 Peter 4.7-11 & Baptised 1 child.
Saturday 24 Meetze, Wingard & myself attended at St. Peters.
Sunday 25 Whitsunday I preached from Gal. 4.6 Father Meetze & myself administered the Sacrament to 70 Communicants & Baptised 1 child. Whit Monday P in Zion from the Gospel St. John 3.16 & Baptised one child.
Sunday the 1 of June P in Zion

Page 51: from the Gospel St. John 3.1-15
Sunday 8 P in Bethlehem from St. Luke 16.19-31.
Sunday 15 at St. Michaels where the Rev. Cook attended and P. from St. Luke 15.2 & Baptised one child.
Sunday 22 P in Zion from the Gospel Luke 15.1-10.
Sunday 29 Smoke & myself P in Nazareth Church I preached from Luke 14.17.
July Sunday the 6 P in Peters Church from Luke 1. Peter 3.12.
Thursday 10 Married John Bouknight to Elizabeth Eliser recd $1
Sunday 13 P in Nazareth Church from the Gospel Mat 5.20 & Baptised 3 Children.
Sunday 20 P at St. Michaels from the Epistle Rom 6.23 & Baptised One child.
Sunday 27 P at Zion Church Preached from the Epistle Rom 8.12
Wednesday 30 P the funeral for John Mathias child from 1 Cor 15.55.
August Sunday 3 P at Peters Church from the Gospel Luke 16.1-9 & Baptised one child & in the afternoon P the funeral for Emanuel Corleys child from Amos 4.12.
Sunday 10 P at Bethlehem from the Gospel Luke 19.41-48.

Page 52: August Saturday 16 P the funeral for Danl Loremans child from 1 Cor 15.55.
Sunday 17. P. at St. Michaels Church from the Gospel Luke 18.9-14.
Sunday 24 P at Zion Church from Rom 10.4 Baptised one child.
Thursday 28 P the funeral for Scotts child from St. John 5.25
Sunday 31 P in Nazareth Church from the Epistle Gal. 3.15. & Baptised 3 children.
Thursday 4 of September Married Daniel Bouknight to Anna Bookman
Sunday 7 P at Peter Church from & in the afternoon at the poor house from John 6.37.
Sunday 21 P at St. Michaels Church from the 32 Psalm verse 1.2. & in the evening commenced a Prayer meeting for the first time.
Sunday 14 P at Bethlehem Church from Mat. 24.12
Sunday 28 P at Zion Church from Mat. 24.29.30.
Sunday the 5 of October P. at Peters Church from 2 Peter 3.14 & on Monday 6 P the funeral for Christina Gable from 1 Cor. 15.55 and in the afternoon at the Poor House.

Page 53: Sunday 12 P. at Nazareth Church from Prov. 29. 1.2.3.
Sunday 19 P. at St. Lukes Church in Edgfield from Prov. 14.12.
Sunday 26 P. at Zion Church from 1 John 3.1 & Baptised 4 Children.
Sunday the 2 of November P. at Peters Church from the Epistle Phil. 1.3-11.
Friday 7 P at Zion Church from the 100 Psalm.
Saturday 8 P. at Nazareth Ch. from Gal. 6.1 & Baptised 1 child.
Sunday 9 P. at Bethlehem Ch. from Gal. 6.1 & Baptised 1 child.
Sunday the 16 P at St. Michaels Church from the epistle Col. 1.9-14 & Baptised 1 child.

I attended the Synod on the 20 of Novr 1828 at St. Johns Church, Charleston.
Sunday 30 P. at Nazareth Church from 1 John 3.1 & Baptised 2 Children.
Thursday the 4 of December Married Henry Koon to Sarah Coogle & Baptised 1 Child.
Sunday 7 P at Peters Church from Prov. 15.12.
Sunday 14 P. the funeral for Jacob Turnipseed from Amos 4.12.
Thursday 18. Married Abraham Frey to Nancy Counts.
Sunday 21 P. at Zion from Phil 2.1-8.

Page 54: Christmas I preached at St. Michaels from Luke 2.32 & Baptised one child. Second Christmas day. Father Meetze & Wingard & myself administered the Sacrament to 50 Communicants at St. Michaels Church.
Sunday 28 P at Bethleham Church from Luke 2.34.
1829 Sunday January 4 P. at St. Peters from Luke 13.8.9 & Baptised 2 children. Sunday 18 P at St. Michaels from 1 John 3.1
Monday 12 Buried Hixes child & P from Amos 4.12 & Baptised 1 child.
Sunday 25 P at Zion Church from Mat 7.
Tuesday 27 Married Saml Halman to Catharine Wingard & Thursday 29 Married Jessee Bouknight to Naomi Metz.
Saturday 30 Buried John Stack & P. from Prov. 14.32.
Sunday the 1 of February P at Peters Church from Prov. 13.6
Sunday 8 P at Bethlehem Ch. from 1 Psalm.
Sunday 15 P at St. Michaels Church from Prov. 10.1-9.
Sunday 22 P at Zion Church from the Gospel Luke 8.5-15.
March 1 P. at Peters Church from Luke 2.34 & Baptised 1 child
March 3 P the funeral

Page 55: of Abraham Stack from Amos 4.12.
Monday 9 P the funeral for John Oxner from the 90 Ps 12.
Sunday 15 P at St. Michaels from Heb. 10.23-25 & Baptised 2 Children.
Sunday 22 P at Zion from the Gospel Luke 11. 21-22 & in the after noon married John Frey to Mary Sherlock. & Baptised 2 Children.
Sunday 29 P at Bethlehem from 2 Tim 3.15.
April Sunday 5 P at Peters Church from 2 Tim 3.15 & Baptised one child.
Sunday 12 P at Bethlehem from
Thursday 16 P at St. Michaels church from the 32 Ps verse

2 & Confirmed 14.
Good Friday the 16 Father Meetze & myself preached I P. from St. John 15.13 & we administered the Sacrament to 70 Comts.
Saturday 18 P at Zion Church St. Luke 22.19 & Confirmed 25 & on Easter Sunday Father Meetze & the Rev. Mealy Preached & we administered the Sacrament to 145 & baptised one child.
Thursday 23 Married Adam Shull to Harriet Lybrand.
Sunday 26 P at Zion from Col. 2. 6.7.
Sunday 3 P. at Peters Church from Acts 16. 30.31

Page 56: Sunday 10 P at Edgefield from 1 Cor. 6.20 & Baptised 4 Children.
Sunday 17 P at St. Michaels from Col. 3.11.
Sunday 24 P at Zion from the Gospel St. John 16.23 & Baptised 1 child.
Ascension Day. P. at Nazareth Ch. from Ephes 4.8
Sunday 31 P. at Bethlehem Ch. from Ephes 4.8.
June Saturday the 6 Wingard & myself P. at Peters Church I P. from 1 Cor. 11. 28 & on Whit Sunday I preached from the gospel St. John 14.25-27. Confirmed 2 Adults & Baptised 3 Children. Communicants 52.
Sunday 14 P at the Church in Edgefield from John 15.13. I then administered the Sacrament to 23 Communicants & baptised 4 Children.
Sunday 21 P. at St. Michaels Church from Luke 16.19-31.
Sunday 28 P. at Zion from Mat 16.26 & baptised 2 children.
Saturday the 4 of July P at St. Michaels from the 100 Ps & the 4 & 5 verse.
Sunday the 5 of July P. at St. Peters from John 3.7 & on Monday the 6. P the funeral for Rev. Rauchs daughter (Julia) from 2 Peter 3.10.11
July 12 P. in Edgefield from John 3.7 & baptised one child & at the same time preached

Page 57: the funeral sermon for old Mr. Rinehart from Amos 4.12.
Sunday 19 P. at Bethlehem Ch. from St. John 3.7 & baptised one child,
Sunday 26 P at Zion Church from John 3.21 & Baptised one child.
August Sunday 2 P at Peters Ch. from Mat 7.21.
Sunday 9 P. at Edgefield Ch. from Mat 7.21
Thursday 13 being a day of humiliation & Prayer appointed by our Synod. I P. at Peters Church from Ps. 51.18 Do good in they good pleasure unto Zion.
Sunday 16 P at St. Michaels from Ps. 19.12 & Baptised one child.
Sunday 23 P at Zion from Mat 7. 13.
Sunday 30 P at Bethlehem Ch. from the Gospel Luke 18.9-14 & Baptised 2 Children.
September 6 P at Peters Ch from
Sunday 13 P at Edgefield from
October 25 P. at St. Michaels Church from St. John 3.16.
Novr 1. P at St. Peters from the Gospel Mat 22.1-14 & Baptised 2 children.
Sunday P at Zion ch. from 2 Cor. 6.2. & Baptised 2 Children.
Sunday 15 P at St. Michaels Church from   & Baptised 1 child.

Page 58: I attended Synod at Savannah on the 20th of November 1829.

Sunday the 29 of Novr P at Zion C. from the Gospel
Mat. 21. 1-9 & Baptised 1 child.
Thursday the 3 of December Married Saml Bouknight to
Mary Coogler.
Sunday the 6 Married David Kyzer to Catharine Hendrix &
P at Peters Church from the Gospel Luke 21.33.
Thursday Decr 10 Married Christian Long to Catharine
Kleckley.
Sunday 20 P at Bethlehem Ch. from Heb. 7.25 & Baptised
2 Children.
Thursday 24 P at St. Michaels Ch. from Mark 1.15 & on
Friday Christmas day Father Meetze & myself P from Mat.
5.6 & we administered the Sacrament to
Sunday 27 P. at Zion Ch. from the gospel Luke 2.33-40
Sunday 3 of January 1830 P. at Peters Ch from   & Baptised 2 children.
Sunday 17 P at St. Michael Ch. from St. John 3.21.
Sunday 24 P. at Zion Ch. from 2 Tim 3.16.17 & Baptised
one child.
Tuesday 26 Buried Mrs. Harman P. from Heb. 9.27
Sunday 31 P. at Nazareth

Page 59: Church from 2 Tim 3,16-17 Baptised 1 Child.
Febry Sunday 14 P at Bethlehem Ch. from 2 Tim 3 16-17.
Sunday 21 P at St. Michaels from Col. 1-14 & Baptised
one child.
Sunday 28 P at Zion from Prov. 22.6.
March 3 Wednesday Buried Gradicks Wife
Thursday 4 Buried Danl Drafts Daughter
Sunday 7 P at St. Peters from 2 Cor 4.3-5
Sunday 14 P at St. Marks from St. John 5.25 it being a
funeral sermon for Jacob Caughmans Wife & Baptised one
child
Sunday 21 P. at St. Michaels from St. James 1.5-7 & Baptised 2 Children
Friday 26 Buried old Christian Long & P from St. John
11.25 & 26.
Sunday 28 P at Zion from 2 Peter 3.1 & Baptised one child.
April Sunday 4 P at St. Peters Church from   & Baptised
one child.
Thursday 8 P at St. Michaels Ch. from St. James 4.7.8.
Goodfriday Father Meetze, Rev. Rauch attended & they P.
after which we administered the Sacrament to 60 Communicants.
Saturday the 10. I preached at Zion Church from St. James
4.7.8.

Page 60: Easter Sunday. Father Meetze & myself P I preached from
2 Cor 5.14.15 & we administered the Sacrament to 112
Communicants & Baptised one child.
Sunday 18 P at Bethlehem Ch from
Sunday 25 P. at Zion Ch. from the Gospel & Baptised 2
children.
Sunday 2 of May P at Peters Church from Phil 3.8.9.
Sunday 9 P at Bethlehem Ch. from Phil 3.8.9.
Friday 14 P the funeral sermon for John Wingards son
from Ps 8.4.
Sunday 16 P at St. Michaels Ch. from Rom. 10.4. & Baptised
4 children.
Sunday 23 P at Zion ch from the Epistle 1 Peter 4.7-11 &
Baptised one child.
Saturday 29. Rev. Stroble & myself attended at Peters

Church I Baptised one Adult & Confirmed 9 Adults. I P. from Gal. 5.22.23 & we administered the Sacrament to 72 Luth & one Meth.
Sunday 6 of June P. at Bethlehem Ch. from the Gospel John 3.1-15.
Sunday 13 P. at Edgefield Ch. from John 1 & 17 & Baptised 2 Children.
Sunday 20 P. at St. Michaels from the Epistle 1 John 3. 3-18 & Baptised one child.
Friday 25 P at Piney woods Ch from Prov. 14.34
Sunday 27 P at Zion Church from Mat. 12.31.32 & Baptised 3 Children.
July Sunday 4 P at St. Peters from Acts 16.30.31

Page 61: Sunday 11 P the Funeral for John Wises Wife from Heb. 4.9.
Sunday 18 P at St. Pauls Ch from Acts 16.30.31.
Sunday 25 P at Zion Ch. from Mat 19.28.
Sunday 1 of August P.at Nazareth Ch. from Act. 16.30.31 Baptised 1 child.
Sunday 8 P at Bethlehem Ch. a Funeral for Anna Hoke who died on the 18 of July.
Thursday 5 Married John Monts to Eliza Turnipseed.
Sunday 15 P at St. Michaels Ch from Acts 5.31 & Baptised one child.
Sunday 22 P. at Zion Church from Luke 18 9-14.
Friday 27 we commenced our three days Meeting at St. Johns Church I Preached from 2 Cor 5.20
Sunday September 5 P at Peters Ch from the gospel Luke 10.23-37 & in the evening married William C. Branham to Anna Gartman.
Sunday 12 P at Bethlehem Ch. from 1 Peter 3.15.
Saturday 11 P the funeral for Daniel Corley from 2 Cor 5.10.
Sunday 19 P at St. Michaels Ch from the Gospel Mat 6. 33 & Baptised one child.
Sunday 26 P at Zion Ch from Rom 8.16 & Baptised one child.
October Sunday 3 P the funeral for Jacob Klecklys Daughter (Sally) from

Page 62: Luke 8. 52 & in the afternoon I buried John Bells child & Br. Stroble P. from Tom 8.18
Sunday 10 P at Nazareth Ch. from John 3.21 & Baptised one child.
Thursday 7 of October married Jessee Tarrer to Miley Huffman
Sunday 17 P at St. Michaels Ch. from Heb 10.35.
Sunday 24 P at Zion Ch from Heb 3.14
Friday, Saturday & Sunday the 29, 30 & 31 attended a Three days meeting at St. Mathews Church Orangeburg.
Sunday the 7 of Novr P at Peters Ch from the gospel Mat. 8. 23-35 & Baptised one Child. & in the afternoon I preached at the C. H. from 1 John 3.1.
Tuesday 9 P the funeral for John Foxes wife from 1 Thes 5.9.10.
Thursday 11 P at St. Michaels Ch from Rom. 10.1
Sunday 14 P at Bethlehem Ch. from Gal. 2.17 & Baptised one child
Thursday 18 P the funeral for Fox child from
Friday 19 attended the Synod at St. Pauls Ch Newberry.

The remainder of missing leaves appearing here should
be between those with September 1826 & December 1827
at top of page. I got them in here by mistake when
resewing this Diary, as it was about to go to pieces
May 1873   J. J. Dreher.

Page 63: Sunday 12 of December P at Bethlehem Ch. from the Gospel.
Sunday 19 P at St. Michaels Ch from the gospel
Christmas day Saturday 25 prevented from Preaching on
account of high water.
Sunday 26 P at Zion Ch from Luke 2 & Baptised one child.
January 1831 Sunday 2 P at St. Peters from Ps 90.10
Baptised one child.
Thursday 6 of January P at Bethlehem from the gospel
Mat 2.1-12 & in the afternoon married William Hoke to
Polly Clark.
Sunday 9 prevented from preaching on account of rain.
Friday 14 Buried Jacob Wingard.
Tuesday 18 Married Jacob Swigard to Elizabeth Wingard.
Thursday 20 Married David Nunemaker to Elizabeth Harman.
Friday 21 Our Three days meeting commenced at St.
Michaels Church.
Sunday 30 P at Zion from Phil 1.21 & Baptised 4 Children.
February 3 Married Joel Bouknight to Catharine W. Ray.

Page 64: Sunday 13 of Febry Preached at Bethlehem Ch. from John
4.24
Sunday 20 P at Nazareth Ch from Prov 14.31 & Baptised 4
children
Sunday 27 P at Zion Ch from Mat 5.48 & Baptised 2 children
Sunday 6 of March P at St. Peters from Rev. 14.13 & Baptised 2 Children & in the after noon married Mcnure to
Elizabeth Rauch.
Wednesday 9 Baptised 3 Children one for John Hendrix,
McGill & Joshua Wingard.
Sunday 13 P at Bethlehem Ch from Titus 3. 5.6.7. Buried
David Haltawangers child.
Sunday 20 P at St. Marks from Titus 3. 5. 6. 7. & Baptised 2 Children.
Sunday 27 P at Zion from Gal. 3. 26.27
Thursday 31 P at Bethlehem from 1 Cor 11. 28 & Confirmed
3 Adults & 10 young persons & on Good Friday I P. from
John 6. 53-54 & administerec the Sacramt to 45 Communicants.

Page 65: Saturday 2 of April Strobel P for me at Zion. I Confirmed 20 young persons & one adult & Baptised 4 Children.
Sunday 3 Easter Sunday I & Father Meetz administered the
Sacrament to 136 Comt.
Sunday 11 P at St. Marks from Luke 24 46.47 & Baptised
one child.

Saturday 16 P at Nazareth Ch from 1 Cor 11.28 & on Sunday 17 I Dedicated Nazareth Ch. after which I P from
John 6. 53.54 & Father Meetze & the Rev. Houck[?] preached
I then confirmed 5 Adults & Father Meetze & Br. Rauch
assisted me in administering the Sacrmt to 46 Communicants
I Baptised 3 Children.
Sunday 24 P at Zion Church from Luke 24.46.47 & Baptised
3 children.
Sunday 1 of May P. at Peters Ch from Rom 5.1. & Baptised
3 children

Saturday 14 P at St. Marks Church from 1 Cor. 11.28
Sunday 15 P from John h.53.54 Confirmed 2 Children administered the Sacrament to 29 Comt & baptised 1 child.

Page 66: Tuesday 17 of May Buried Mrs. Rauch & P from 1 Cor 15.19 & in the after noon Buried Edwin Scotts child & P from 2 Cor 4.17
Saturday 21 P at Peters Ch from Mat 5.4
Sunday 22 Whit Sunday Father Rall & myself P I preached from Acts 2.4 Confirmed 3 Adults, Rall & myself administered the Sacrament to 68 Luth & 4 Meths. I baptised one adult & one child.
Sunday May 29 P at Nazareth Ch from the gospel St. John 3.1-15 & in the afternoon P at Lexington C. H. from Heb. 4.1.
Sunday 4 of June P at Zion Ch from Heb. 11.1 & in the afternoon P at Lexington C. H. from Rom. 10.4
Sunday 12 P at St. Jacobs Ch from Rom 10.4
Sunday 19 P at St. Marks Edgefield from the gospel Luke 15.1-10
Sunday 26 P at Zion Ch from the gospel Luke 6.36-45 & in the afternoon at the Court House from Acts 16.30.31.

Page 67: Sunday 3 of July in the morning 8 oclock buried Young George Wingard & P from 1 Peter 1.24 Then at Peters Church from the Epistle 1 Peter 3.8-15 & Baptised 2 children & in the after noon at the C. H. from Rom 6.22
Sunday 10 P at Bethlehem from Rom 6.22
Monday 11 P the funeral for young George Lykes from Ecclesiastes 12.1
Sunday morning the 17 Married John Wise to Catharine Elizabeth Rinehart & P at St. Marks Ch from the Epistle Rom 6.22 & in the afternoon P a funeral sermon for one of Col. Bates sons from Heb. 4.9.
Sunday 24 P at Zion Ch from the epistle Rom 8.12-17 & Baptised 2 Children & in the afternoon attended a prayer meeting in the fork.
Friday 29 Rauch & myself attended a three days meeting at Sandyrun I P from Rom 8.1 & Rauch from Heb 4.16 on Saturday 30 Scheek P from Isa 55.6 & Schwartz from Luke 22.19
Sunday morning 30 I P from 1 Cor 1.21 & Schwartz from Isa 1.2 & Schick from Gal. 6.7 after which I Confirmed Four adults & we administered the Sacrament
Sunday 7 of August I P at Peters Ch

Page 68: from the gospel Luke 19.41-48 & Baptised one child & in the afternoon I P at the Court House from 1 Cor 1.18.
August 14 P at Nazareth Ch from Rom 8.1 & Baptised 3 Adults in the afternoon I P at the C. H. from Heb. 2.3
Wednesday 17 Baptised Fed Harmons child & on Friday 19 Baptised Miss Floids child
Sunday 21 P at St. Marks from Rom 8.1 after preaching I married Jacob Caughman to Elizabeth Derick in the afternoon I P at Longs Ch from Heb. 2.3.
Sunday 28 P the Funeral for Rev. J. Schwartz from Rev. 14.13
Saturday the 3 of Septr P for Br. Schick from Luke 18.13 & on Sunday the 4 I P. from Acts 16.31.32 & Baptised his daughter & we administered the Sacrament
Tuesday 6 Br. Moser & myself attended the Buriel of two of George Addys sons I P. from Heb. 2.6.

Sunday morning 11 P. the Funeral for Mathias Cooglers son from Heb. 2.6. & Baptised one child.
Sunday 11 oclock P. at Bethlehem Ch from Rev. 14.18 & Baptised one child.

Page 69: Saturday 17 of September P at Stoney battery Ch from 1 Cor 1.21 & Baptised one child.
Sunday 18 P at St. Marks Ch Edgefield from Rev. 14.13 & in the afternoon P at Longs Ch from 1 Cor 1.21 & baptised one child.
Sunday 25 P at St. Peters Ch from Rev. 2.10 & Baptised 2 Children.
Thursday 29 buried on of Gabriel Hoylers children & P from Heb 9.27 & in the afternoon buried on of John Loremans sons & P from Rev. 2.10 & on Saturday Baptised Countses child.
Sunday the first of October P in Zion Ch from Rev. 14.13 & baptised 1 child.
Friday the 7 P the funeral for Benj. Roofs Wife from Rom 5.18
Sunday the 9 P at Nazareth Ch from 2 Cor 5.14 & Baptised one child.
Sunday 16 P at St. Marks from 2 Cor 5.18 & Baptised one child.
Monday 17 Buried Daniel Amicks Wife & P from Rom 5.18
Our four days meeting commenced at Lexington C. H. on the 27 of October I confirmed 2 Adults
The Four days meeting in Newbery Bethlehem Ch I Baptised one adult & Confirmed two persons.
Sunday 13 P at Bethlehem Ch from Prov. 23.26 & Baptised one child.
Saturday 19 P at St. Lukes Ch from 2 Thes 2.12.13
Sunday 20 P at St. Marks Ch from Ps. 1912 & Confirmed 3 adults

Page 69: December Sunday 4 P at Zion Ch from Rom 14.7.8 & Baptised one child.
Tuesday 6 Buried old Mrs. Bouknight P from Rev. 7.14
Friday 9 attended the Synod at Sandy run
Sunday the 11 Confirmed 3 Persons
Friday the 16 P St. Lukes Ch from Rom 10.1 Baptised 2 Children
Saturday I P at St. Marks Ch from Mat 5.4
Sunday the 18 P from Mat 11.28. Baptised 2 adults & Confirmed 1 & administered the Sacrament.
Saturday 24 P at Zion Ch from Mat 5.4 & on Christmas Sunday I P from the gospel Luke 2 & administered the sacrament & Baptised one child
Monday 26 P at St. Michaels Ch from Titus 2.11-14 & in the afternoon Buried Emanuel Geigers child & P from Rev. 14.13
Sunday the 1 of January 1832 P at St. Michaels from the Epistle Gal. 3.23-29
Sunday 8 P at St. Johns Church from the epistle Rom 12.1-6 & Baptised one child
Epiphany the 6 of Jany P at Zion Ch from Luke 2.32
Sunday 15 P at St. Marks Ch from Mat 12.31.32
Saturday 21 P at St. Michaels Ch Rev. Hope P & on Sunday 22

Page 70: Rev. Haltiwanger P & I administered the Sacrament & on Sunday afternoon I P the funeral for McNures wife from Ps 34.19

Friday 27 I attended a Three days meeting at St. Johns Church I P from 1 Tim 1:15
on Sunday 29 I Dedicated the Ch. & P from Luke 10,30-37
Sunday 5 of Feby P at Peters Ch from the gospel Mat 13. 24-30.
Thursday 9 Married Daniel Kleckly to Barbara Drafts.
Sunday 12 P at Bethlehem Ch from Mat 13.24-30 & Baptised One child.
Sunday 19 P at St. Johns from the Gospel & Baptised 3 Children.& in the after noon Buried one.
Thursday 23 Married Martin Caughman to Kiza Wise.
Sunday 26 prevented from preaching in consequence of rain & sleat.
Friday, Saturday & Sunday the first of March Haltawanger Myself & others attended at Nazareth Ch I P on Sunday on Baptism & Baptised 4 children. & confirmed one & administered the Sacrament.
Sunday 11 P at St. Marks from the gospel
Thursday 8 Married Noah Roberts to Rebecca Kelly
Sunday 18 P at St. Johns from the gospel & baptised one child
Sunday 25 P at St. Michaels from the gospel & baptised

Page 71: 2 children.
Sunday 1 of April P at St. Peters Ch from John 8.47
Sunday 8 P at Zion Ch from
Sunday 15 P at St. Johns from Mat 9.13 & Baptised 1 Child
Good Friday P at Zion from 1 Cor 2.2 & baptised 1 child & on Easter Sunday I P from Rom 6.9-11
Easter Monday I attended at Bethlehem & P from the epistle Acts 10.43 & baptised one child
Sunday 29 P at Bethlehem from the gospel John 20.19
May Sunday 6 P in Zion Church & baptised 1 child.
Sunday 13 P at St. Marks Edgefield from Rom 10.4 & baptised 1 child & on Monday buried Allen Waites child
Sunday 20 prevented from preaching an account of Sickness
Sunday 27 P at St. Michaels Ch from Rom 10.4 & baptised 1 child
Sunday 3 of June P at Peters Ch & baptised 1 child
Ascension day P at Bethlehem Ch from Ephes 4.8 baptised 1 child
Saturday 10 P from 1 John 1.8.9. & on Sunday being Whitsuntide I P from Acts 2.4. & administered the Sacrament to 37 Communicants.

Page 72: Sunday 17 P at St. Johns ch from Rom 10.4 & baptised 1 child
Saturday 23 Haltawanger & myself P at St. Michaels Ch I P from Prov. 28.13 & on Sunday the 24 I P from Luke 18.9-14 & administered the Sacrament to 62 Communicants & Confirmed one adult.
Saturday & Sunday the 14.15 P at St.Marks from 1 John 1.8.9. & on Sunday P from Luke 18.9-14 & administered the Sacrament to 33 Comt & Baptised 4 Children on Saturday the 14 Baptised Do. **Todds** [?] Child & one black child.
The first July I P at Zion Church from Gal. 2.17
Sunday 15 P at St. Johns from Luke 19.10 & baptised one child & on Thursday the 19 P at Johns Ch from 147 Ps 5-14 it being the day appointed by the Synod it

was well attended to by a large Congregation after preaching baptised Galmans Child.
Friday 29 of June Buried Christena Mathias & P from Heb. 4.9.

Page 73: Sunday 22 P at St. Michaels Ch from Luke 19.10 & baptised Fed Wises child
Friday Saturday & Sunday the 27.28.29 & 30 at St. Johns Ch. near Jacob Rawls
Wednesday the 8 of August buried Saml Huffmans wife & P from Rev. 7.14
Sunday 12 P in Nazareth Ch from Rom 6. 23 & Baptised 5 Children.
Saturday 18 P in St. Johns from 1 Cor 11.28.29 & on Sunday P from the Gospel Luke 16.1-9 & administered the Sacrament to 60 Comts & baptised 6 children
Sunday 26 P in Zion Ch from the Epistle 1 Cor 12.1-11 & Baptised one child & in the afternoon P at Lexington C. H. from Mat 9.12.
September Saturday L P at St. Pauls Ch Hollow Creek from 1 Cor 11.28.29 & on Sunday I P from the Gospel Luke 18.9-14 & Confirmed 3 Persons & administered the Sacrament
Sunday 9 P in Piney Woods Ch from the Epistle 2 Cor 3.4-11 & Bapitsed 3 Children & on Monday I P from John 10.5 & on Tuesday from Luke 16.31 & Confirmed 5 Persons
Sunday 16 P at St. Johns from the epistle Gal. 6. & Baptised 2 Children

Page 74: Saturday 22 Buried George Roberts Child & Preached from 2 Cor 4.1
on Sunday 23 P at Longs Church from Gal. 6.
Sunday 30 attended a 3 days meeting at Stoney Battery Ch
Wednesday 3 of October attended at Rineharts Ch & baptised 3 children
on Sunday 7 of October attended a 3 days meeting at Edisto
Sunday 14 Buried George Harmans daughter Rebecca & P at Zion Ch from Mat 16.26 & baptised 1 child
sunday 21 P at St. Johns from St. Marks Gospel 16.15.16 on Friday attended a 3 days meeting at Lexington C. H. & in the afternoon P the funeral for Andrew Summers child from Heb 9.27 & on Tuesday commenced a 3 days meeting at Zion Ch & Baptised 3 children
Friday 26 attended a 3 days meeting at Bethlehem Ch Newberry.
I Attended the synod at St. Mathews Ch Orangeburge on the 17 Nov 1832
Sunday 25 P in St. Michaels Ch from the Gospel   & Baptised 1 child
Sunday 9 P in Zion Ch from 2 Peter 3.1 & baptised 2 children
Sunday 16 P at St Johns Ch from 2 Peters 3.7 & in the afternoon Preached

Page 75: the funeral for George A. Koons Wife at Peter Buzzards from Heb. 4.9.
Buried My Br. Jesse on Saturday the 8 of Decr 1832
Sunday 23 P at St. Michaels from the Gospel & baptised 1 Child & on Tuesday (Christmas) P at Bethlehem from the Gospel & baptised 1 child & on Thursday the 27 buried

Christian Weeds child P fromHeb. 4.9
Sunday 30 P at Longs Ch from Luke 2.9 & Baptised 5 children.
Sunday the 6 of January 1833 P at Peters Ch
Saturday 12 P the funeral for Daniel Metz child from Mat 18.3 & on Sunday 13 P at St. Mathews Ch in Hopes place
Sunday 20 P at St. Johns from Rom 8.2 & on Thursday the 24 Married Rev. John C. Hope to Luesia Eigleberger & on Sunday the 27 P at St. Michaels from Rom 8.2. & baptised 1 child & on Thursday the 31 the day appointed by the Convention I P at Zion Ch from James 4.10 & Baptised 2 children.
Sunday 3 of Febry P at Zion Ch from Rom 8.3 & baptised 2 children

Page 76: Thursday 7 Married Daniel Bookman to Sally Derick
Sunday 10 P at Egners Ch in Newberry from St. Mark 16.15.16
Sunday 17 Prevented on account of rain
Sunday 24 P at St. Michaels Ch from 1 John 3 &
Sunday 3 of March P at zion Ch from the Gospel
Thursday 25 Buried old Mrs. Metze & P from Heb. 13.14
Sunday 10 P at Bethlehem Ch from the Gospel Luke 11.14-28 & Baptised one child
Tuesday 12 P the funeral for George Wises Wife from 1 Cor 15.55
Sunday 17 P at St. Johns Ch from the Gospel Gal. & Baptised 1 child
Thursday 21 of March Married Saml Huffman to Sally Derick
Sunday 24 P at St Michaels from 2 Cor 13.5
Sunday 31 P at Zion Ch from   & baptised 2 Children.
April Thurday 4 P in St. Michaels Ch from Acts 8. & Confirmed 11 Persons & baptised 2 children
on Goodfriday Rauch & myself preach & administered the Sacrament & I P from Mat 26.21

Page 77: on Saturday 6 April I P in Zion Ch from Acts 8.17 & Confirmed 19 Persons.
On Easter Sunday prevented on account of rain
Sunday 14th prevented on account of sickness
Sunday 21 P at St Johns from the gospel John 10.11-18 & baptised 3 children
Sunday 28 P at St. Michaels from Gal. 5.1
Sunday 5 of May P at Zion Ch from the gospel John 16.5-15 & in the afternoon administered the Sacrament to old Mr Frey & his wife
Wednesday the 8th P old Father Meetzes funeral from Job 7.1-4
Saturday 11 P at Peters Ch from 2 Cor 13.15 & on Sunday the 12.I P from Mat 26.26 & confirmed 2 persons & administered the Sacrament to about 30 persons & baptised one child
Saturday 18 of May P in Zion Ch from 116 Ps v 12-14 & also on Sunday 19 I P again from Mat 26.26-28 & baptised one adult & one child & confirmed 7 Persons & administered the Sacrament to about 140 Communicants.

Page 78: May 16 being Ascension day P in St. Johns Ch from the gospel Mark 16 & baptised 3 children
Saturday 25 of May P at St. Johns Ch from Ps 116 12-14 &

Confirmed 14 Persons & on Sunday the 26 being Whitsunday I P from Mat 26.26-28 & administered the Sacrament to 74 Communicants
Tuesday 28 of May 1833 Married Henry Chalmers to Elisabeth Weed
Sunday 2 of June P at Zion Ch from the gospel John 3. 1-14 & in the after noon at Lexington C. H. from Numbers 22.18 & baptised 1 child
Sunday 16 P at St. Johns from the gospel Luke 14.14-26 & baptised 1 child & on Tuesday 18 of June P the funeral for Adam Roberts child from Luke 8.52
Sunday 23 of June P in St. Michaels Ch from the gospel Luke 15
Thursday 27 of June Married Sanders Swigard to Harriet Lorick & on Sunday the 30 of June attended a baptist meeting near spring hill.
Sunday 7 of July P at Zion Ch from the Epistle 1 Peter 3.12 & baptised 2 children & in the afternoon preached the funeral of Mrs. _____

Page 79: from 1 Cor 15.55
The 14 of July P at St. Peters Ch from the gospel
Thursday the 18 of July being the day appoitned by the Synod I attended at St. Michaels Ch from 147 Ps & the 5-14 & on Sunday the 21 P at St. Johns Ch from the gospel St Mark 8.1-9 & baptised 1 child
Thursday the 25 of July 1833 Married Joel Corley to Juda Cauley & on Sunday the 28 P the funeral for Hixes child from Mat 24.44 & at the same time attended a meeting of five days at St. Johns Ch near Ralls & Leaphart
Sunday the 4 of August P in Zion Ch from the gospel Luke 16.1-9 & in the after noon attended a Prayer meeting at David Kleckleys & P from 34 Ps 19 verse
Sunday the 18th attended a three days meeting near Spring Hill
Friday the 23 of August Preached the funeral for old Mrs. Geiger from 2 Kings 20.1 & on Sunday the 25 P in St. Michaels Ch from Gal. 3.11 & on Tuesday the 27 of August P the Funeral for George Robertses wife from St. John 3.36
Sunday the 1 of September P at Edisto Ch from Mark 16. 16 & Baptised one child & on Thursday the 5 of Septr Buried David Kleckly & P from Prov. 14.32 & on Saturday the 7 of Septr P at Longs Ch from 1 Cor 11 & on Sunday I P from John 6. 53 & administered to 15 persons & baptised 2 children
Sunday the 15 of Septr P at St Johns Ch from the gospel Mat 6.24-34
Sunday 22 of Septr P in St Michaels ch from 1 Cor 15.1.2 & on Wednesday 25 P the funeral for Adam Chapman from Prov 14.32 & on Sunday 29 of Septr P in Bethlehem Ch from Gal. 6.14 & on the 2 of October P the funeral for Henry Seastrunk from Rev. 14.13
Sunday 6 of October P in Zion Ch from the gospel Mat 22.34-46 & baptised 1 child in the afternoon attended prayer meeting at old Mr Galles & baptised 1 child & on Monday the 7 of October P the funeral for Daniel Kleckleys child from Luke 18.16.17 & baptised 1 child
Sunday the 13 of October P at St Marks Ch in Edgefield & baptised one adult & 2 children & Confirmed 3 persons & on Monday the 14 buried Michael Kinard & P from 1 Thes 5.9

Sunday 20 P at St Johns from the gospel Mat 22.1-14
Thursday 24

Page 80: P the funeral for Simion Addys child from 1 Thes 5.9
Friday 25 P the funeral for G Heylers child from 2 Peter 3.11
Sunday 27 P at St Michaels Ch from Gal. 6.1-10 & baptised 1 child Saturday the 2 of Novr 1833 P at St. Johns from Gal. 6.1-10 & baptised 3 children & in the afternoon P the funeral for Capt Millers son from Ps 8.4
Sunday morning Nov 3 Married John Mathias to Susanna Tarrer & from there we went to Zion Church & heard the Rev. Hanes for the first time & I baptised 3 children
Saturday the 9 I P at Edisto Church Mount Calvary from 2 Cor 5.20 & on Sunday I P from St. John 6.53 Confirmed one, baptised 2 children & administered the Sacrament to 36.
Sunday the 16 of November 1833 attended the Synod at Lexington village.

Page 81: Saturday 23 of November P the funeral for John Chapmans wife from 2 Cor 4.17.18.
Sunday 24 I P in St. Michaels form 2 Peter 3.18
Sunday the first of Decr I P at Zion Ch from 2 Peter 3.18 & baptised one child
Sunday the 15 of Decr P at St Johns Ch from the epistle 1 Cor 4.1-5 baptised one child & in the afternoon P the funeral for old Mrs. John Counts from Rev. 14.13
Saturday the 21 P the funeral for old Mr. Gable from Job 7.2
Sunday 22 P at St Michaels Ch from Acts 20.32 & baptised one child
Christmas day I attended at Zion Ch where Dr. Hazelious & Mr. Hope preached & baptised 3 children
Thursday the 2 of January 1834 Married Michael Drafts to Mary Younginer,
Sunday 12 of January P at St Johns Church from The Epistle Rom 12.1-2
Sunday 19 P at Zion Church from the gospel John 2.1-11 & Baptised 1 child
Saturday the 18 P at St Jacobs Church from Acts 4.12
Sunday 26 P at St Johns Ch from the gospel Mat 20.1-16 & baptised 3 children
Sunday the 3 of February I P at St Peters Church Piney Woods from the Gospel Luke 8.4-15 & baptised six children & on Thursday the 6 of February I Married William Sweetenberg to Harriet Summer

Page 82: Sunday the 9 of February 1834 P at St. Johns from the Epistle 1 Cor 13.
Wednesday the 12 of February Married John N. Summer to Nancy Suber & on Thursday the 13 of February Married Henry Craps to Adah Addy.
Monday the 10 February P the Funeral for old Mrs. Tayler from Rev. 14.13 & on Sunday the 16 P at Zion Ch from 1 Thes 5.17
Sunday the 23 P in St Johns from the Gespel Epistle 1 Thes 4.1.
Saturday the 15 P in St Jacobs Church from 1 Cor. 1.21
The first Sunday in March P at St Peters Ch Pineywoods

from the gospel Luke 11.14
Sunday the 9 of March P at St Johns from Col. 1.14
Sunday the 16 of March P at Zion Ch from Col. 1.14
Thursday the 20 of March Married William Summer to Christena Hip
Sunday the 23 P at St Johns Ch from Rom 8.3.
Thursday the 27 P at Zion Ch from 1 Cor 11.28 & in the afternoon Married Henry Metz to Nancy Suldon
on Goodfriday I was prevented from preaching on account of the rain
On Saturday I attended a four days meeting at Bethel Ch & Preached from Ephes 4.5. & On Easter Sunday I again preached from Col. 3.1. & on Easter

Page 83: monday I P at St Peters Ch in the pineywoods & P from the epistle Acts 10 & the following gentlemen were elected the committee for building the new Church Jacob Wheeler, Jacob Mayer, Harman, Sease & Bowers.
Sunday the 6 of April I P at St Peters Ch from the gospel & on Sunday the 13 I P at St Johns Ch from the Epistle 1 Peter 2.21 & Tuesday the 15 married George Adam Koon to Sarah Cromer & on Friday the 18 buried Adam Mayer & P from 34 Ps 19 & on Saturday the 19 P at St Jacobs Ch from Titus 3.5.6.
Sunday the 20 of April P at Zion Ch from Luke 22.10 & administered the Sacrament of the Lords Supper to 95 Communicants & baptised one child
Monday 21 buried Adam Wingard & P from Ps 34.19 & on Tuesday buried Thomas Slighs Son & P from Ps 39.4.5.6.
Sunday 27 P at St John from the epistle James 1.16-21 & baptised one child
Saturday the 3 of May I P at St Peters Ch from 1 Cor 11.28 & Confirmed 12 persons & Baptised 1 adult & 5 children & on Sunday the 4 P from St Luke 22.19 & administered the Sacrament to 105 Persons.

Page 84: Thursday 8 of May being Ascension day I P at Bethlehem Ch on broad River from the gospel Mark 16.14.
Sunday 11 of May P at St Johns Ch from ps 119.9 & in the afternoon preached the funeral for John Fulmer from Ps 39.4 & Baptised 3 children
Saturday the 17 of May P at St Johns Ch from Luke 22.19 & in the afternoon Buried one of John Fulk's children & on Sunday being Whit Sunday I P from Luke 14.17 Confirmed 2 Persons & administered the Sacrament to about 81 Communicants.
Whit Monday the Rev. Moser & myself P at St Jacob's I P from the gospel St John 3.16-21 & baptised 2 children.
Sunday the 25 of May I P at Zion Ch from the gospel St John 3.1-15
Sunday the 1 of June I P in St Peters Ch pineywoods from the gospel Luke 16.19-31 & baptised 1 child
Sunday the 8 of June I P in St. Johns Ch from the epistle 1 John 3.13-18 & baptised 4 children
Friday 13 buried Jacob Nunnemakers son Lavall & P from 1 Cor 15.22 & on Saturday the 14 I P at St. Jacobs Ch from Luke 15.1-10

Page 85: Sunday the 15 the Dr. & myself attended at Zion Ch
Sunday 22 P at St Johns Ch from Luke 18.13
Saturday 21 P at Bethlehem Broad River Luke 18.13.
Wednesday 25 Buried Capt Wise's child Mary Cat & P

from Rev. 14.13
Sunday the 6 of July P in St Peters Ch piney woods from the gospel Mat 5.20 & baptised 2 children
Tuesday the 15 Buried the widow Senn & P from Heb 4.9.
Sunday the 13 P at St John's Ch from the gospel Mark 8. 1-9.
Sunday 20 P. at Zion from the gospel Mat 7.15-21 & baptised one child
Saturday the 19 P. at St. Jacobs Ch from the gospel Mat 7.15-21 & baptised one child.
Saturday 26 P in Bethlehem Ch Broad River from Rom 10. 4 & on Sunday 27 P at St John's Ch from the gospel Luke 16.1-9 & baptised 1 child
July Monday 28 Buried Nicholas Sligh's son & preached from Heb 4.9
Thursday 31 of July Married Saml Byers to Harriet Nunemaker
Sunday 3 P at St Peters Ch piney woods from the Epistle 1 Cor 12.1-11 & baptised 2 children
Sunday Augt the 10. P. at St. John's from 1 Cor 15.1-10 & baptised 2 children
Saturday 16 P at St. Jacobs Ch from the Epistle 2 Cor 3.4-11 & baptised 1 child
Sunday 17 P at Zion Ch from the Epistle 2 Cor 3.4-11 & baptised 2 children recd $30

Page 86: Tuesday 19 Buried John Fullmers daughter & preached from Luke 8.52 & on Wednesday the 20 August
Buried old Mrs Bales & P from Heb 4.9 & on Saturday 23 P in Bethlehem Ch from Col 1.28 & on Sunday 24 of August P. St. John's Ch from the Gospel Luke 10.23-37 & on Wednesday 27 Buried George Eptings wife & P. from Heb. 4.9.
August Sunday 31 P at Bethlehem Ch Broad River from the Epistle Gal. 5.16-24.
Sunday the 7 of Septr P. at St. Peters Ch piney woods from the epistle Gal. 6.1-10 & baptised 2 children & on Sunday the 14 P. at St. Johns from the gospel Luke 7.11-17.
Saturday 27 P at Bethlehem Ch from Math 22.34-46.
Sunday 28 P at St Johns from the gospel Mat 22.34-46 & baptised 2 children
Sunday 5 of October P. at St. Peters Ch piney woods from the gospel Mat 9.1-8 & baptised 2 children
Sunday the 12 of October I P. at St. Johns Ch from the gospel Mat 22.1-14 on Saturday the 11 I P at Bethlehem Ch Broad River from Mat 22.14

Page 87: Saturday the 18. of October 1834. P. at St. Jacobs Ch from the gospel John 4.47-54 & baptised 1 child
Sunday the 19 P at Zion Ch from the gospel St John 4.47-54 & baptised 1 child
Monday the 20 I P the funeral for Baruch Gregory from Luke the 23. 42-43 & baptised 2 children
Sunday the 4 in October P. in St. Johns Ch & on the first Sunday in November P. in Piney woods Church from the gospel & baptised 2 children & on Friday Buried Daniel Metzs Wife & Preached from Ps 89.15 & on the second Saturday in Novr preached in Bethlehem Ch & on the second Sunday in Novr P the funeral for old George Summer from Luke 23. 42.43

Synod

Thursday 27 of November 1834 Married Buff to Rachel Mathias
Sunday the 30 P. at St. Johns Ch from the gospel & baptised 2 children
Thursday the 4 of Decr started to N. C. & returned on Saturday the 20 & on Sunday 21 P at Zion Ch & on Christmas I P again at Zion & on Second Christmas day I Preached at Bethlehem on Broad River & on Tuesday the first of January 1835 I P at St. Peters piney woods from Titus 3.4-7 & in the afternoon I buried William Holman & P from Job. 14.14
Sunday 11 of January P at St. Johns Ch from the gospel Luke 2. 41-52 & in the afternoon buried old Mr. Wheeler & preached from Heb. 4.9

Page 88: January 17 1835. P. at Bethlehem Ch from Titus 3.4-7 & baptised one child recd $5
Preached at St Johns on the 25 of Jany & baptised 1 child & recd $35
Sunday the 1 of Feby P at St Peters Ch from the gospel Mat 8. 27-30 & baptised 4 children
Tuesday 10 of Febry P. the funeral of Old Squire Bayle from John 11.25
Saturday 14 P at Bethlehem from Mat 13.24-30 & baptised one child & on Sunday the 15 P at Zion Ch from the gospel Mat 20.1-16 & baptised one child
Sunday 22 P at St. Johns Ch from the gospel Luke 8.4-15 recd $42
Sunday the first of March in St Peters from the gospel Luke 18.31-43 & baptised 3 children.
Sunday the 8 of March the snow fell.
Sunday the 14 P in Zion Ch from the gospel Mat 15.21-28 & baptised 2 children
on Thursday the 12 of March Buried John Mathias Wife
Sunday the 22 of March P at St Johns Ch from the gospel Luke 11. 14-28
Thursday the 26 of March Married Daniel Metz

Page 89: to Presilla Weed. & baptised 2 children
Sunday 29 of March P the funeral semon for Jacob Earharts Daughter from Luke 8.
Sunday the 5 of April P at Piney woods ch from the gospel   & baptised 3 children & on Sunday 12 P at St. Johns Ch from the Epistle Phil 2.5-11 & baptised 4 children & recd $20.
goodfriday P at Bethlehem Ch from Isa 53.
Saturday 18 P at Zion Ch from 1 John 1.9. & baptised one child & on Easter Sunday I P. from Col 3.1 & administered the Sacrament to 107 Communicants
On Thursday the 23 of April Married Jesse Hufman to Malinda Tarrer
Sunday the 26 P at St Johns from the gospel St. John 20.19-31 & in the afternoon I P. the funeral for Mrs. Stone from St. John 5.24
Sunday the 3 of May P in St. Peters Ch from the gospel St John 10.11-16 & baptised 3 children

Page 90: Wednesday the 6 of May 1835. Buried Saml Byers wife & Preached from 2 Cor 4.18
Sunday the 10 of May P. at St. Johns Ch from the gospel John 16.15-22 & baptised 3 children

Sunday the 17 P at Zion Ch from the gospel John 16.
5-15
Thursday the 7 of May Married David Roof to Nancy Gable.
Sunday 24 P at St. Johns Ch frpm the Gospel St. John
15 & 16
Thursday the 4 of June 1835 Married Dr. Souter to Luesia
Bernhardt
Saturday the 6 of June I P. at St. Peters Ch Piney woods
from 1 John 1.9 & on Sunday I P. from the gospel John
14.23-31 & administered the Sacrament to 105 Comts &
baptised one child
Thursday the 11 of June Married David Fulmer to Amey
Wessinger & in the afternoon Buried old Mrs. Lindler
& P from Job 7.1.2.3. & baptised 2 children

Page 91: Saturday 13 P at St Johns Ch from 1 John 1.9 & baptised
one adult & Confirmed 22 Persons & on Sunday the 14 P.
from the gospel St John 3.1-15 & administered the Sa-
crament to 109. $8
June Sunday 21 P at Zion Church from the gospel Luke
16 & baptised one child
Thursday 25 buried Capt. Millers child & preached from
Luke 8.52
Sunday the 28 of June P. at St. Johns Ch from the gos-
pel Luke 14.16-24 & baptised 3 children
Sunday the 5 of July P at St. Peters Ch from the gospel
Luke 15.1-15
Thursday the 9 P the funeral for old Mrs. Miller & two
of her sons children from Rom 8.18
Sunday July 12 P at St Johns Ch from the epistle Rom 8.
18-23
Saturday the 18 of July P at Bethlehem Ch from Gol. 3.
26 & baptised one child & on Sunday the 19. P. in Zion
Ch from the Epistle 1 Peter 3.8-15 & baptised 2 children
The next N. C. Synod will meet on the 3 Sunday in May.
Pilgrim's Ch Davidson County
Sunday 26 P at St Johns Ch from the Gospel Mat 5.20-26

Page 92:   1835
Sunday the 2 of August P. in St. Peters Ch from the
gospel Mark 8.1-9
Sunday the 9 of August P in St. Johns Ch from the gospel Mat 7.15-23 & baptised one child & on Saturday the
15 P at Bethlehem Ch from 1 John 3.1.2.
Sunday 16 P at Zion Ch from the Gospel 16.1-9 & baptised
one child
Sunday 23 P at St Johns from the Epistle 1 Cor 12.1-11
Saturday the 29 P at St Pauls Ch little Hollowcreek from
1 John 1.9 & on Sunday the 30 I P from 1 Cor 2.2 & admst.
the Sacrament to   & baptised 1 child
September Sunday the 6 P at St Peters Ch piney woods
from the epistle 2 Cor 3.4-11
Sunday the 13 P at St Johns Ch from the gospel Luke 10.
23-37 & baptised 2 children
Tuesday the 15 of Septr I buried old Mrs Long or as she
was generally called old Mrs Kleckly & P from John 5.24
Thursday the 17 Married John Wise to Christena Geiger
Saturday the 19 P at Bethlehem Ch from Gal. 2.20 &
baptised 1 child
Sunday 20 P at Zion Ch from the epistle Gal. 5.16-24
Sunday 27 P at St Johns Ch from the epistle Gal. 6.1-10

Page 93: & baptised one child
Thursday 24 of Septr 1835 Married Samuel Lorick to Nancy Kaigler
Sunday the 4 of October P at St Peters Ch Piney woods
Sunday the 11 of October P at St Johns Ch from the epistle Ephes 4.1-6 on Tuesday the 13 Buried Capt George Miller & P from John 5.24 & on Thursday the 15 of Oct Married Richard Scott to Caroline Ellenbarg
Sunday the 18 of Octr P at Zion Ch from 1 John 3.23.24
Sunday the 25 P & attended St Johns Ch & Harman Aull preached & I baptised one child
Wednesday the 28 baptised Sousen Weeds child
Sunday the first of November 1835 P at St Peters Ch from the gospel Mat 22.1-14 & baptised 6 children.
Sunday the 8 P at St Johns Ch from the gospel John 4.47
Thursday the 12 Married John Buff to Rachal Hook & baptised 1 child
Sunday the 15 at Zion & Rankins the Reformed Minister Preached

Page 94: Attended the Synod Novr 1835
Sunday the 22 of Novr Scheck P for me at St Johns Church
Sunday the 29 Dr. Hazelius & myself Dedicated St Peters Ch in the Pineywoods & I baptised 3 children
Wednesday the 2 of December Married S. H. Smith to my daughter Nancy
Thursday 3 Married Eliza Auston to Julian Sulton
Sunday the 6 P at Bethlehem Ch from 1 Tim 1.15
Sunday the 13 P at St Johns Ch from the gospel Mat 11.2-10 & baptised one child
Sunday the 20 P at Zion Ch from the gospel St John 1.10-28 & baptised 2 children
Christmas Day I P at St. Peters Ch Pineywoods & P from the Gospel Luke 2.1-14 & baptised 3 children & on Second Christmas day I P. at Zion Ch from Luke 2.1-14
Sunday the 27 P at Salem Ch upper Hollow Creek from the Epistle Gal. 4.1-7 & baptised 1 child
The first Sunday in January 1836 P at St. Peters from the epistle Titus 3.4-7 & baptised one child
Epiphany I P at St Johns from the gospel Mat 2.1-12
The first Sunday after Epiphany I P at St Peters Piney woods from the epistle Rom 12.1-6 & baptised one child
Sunday the 17 P at Zion Ch from Gal. 4.6 & baptised one child

Page 95: Thursday the 21 of January Married Godfrey Geiger to Elizabeth Easter Lorick
Sunday the 24 Prevented on account of Sleet & on Sunday the 31 prevented on account of rain
Monday the first of February buried Daniel Bouknight & preached from Heb. 4.9
Sunday the 7 of Feb P at Piney woods Ch from the gospel Mat 13.24-30 & baptised 3 children
Thursday the 11 of Feby Married John Mathias to Barbara Weed & baptised one child
Sunday the 14 P at St Johns Ch from the gospel Luke 18.31-43 & baptised 3 children
Monday 15 Buried old Mrs Rister & preached from Mat 24-44 & baptised one child   Saturday the 20 P at Bethlehem Ch from 34.19
Sunday the 21 of Febry P in Zion Ch from the Epistle

2 Cor 6.1-10 & baptised one child.
Thursday the 25 Married Conrad Senn to Selena Book
Saturday the 27 baptised 2 children for John Earigle &
on Sunday prevented from preach on account of the cold
& rain
Sunday the 6 of March P at St Peters Ch pineywoods from
the gospel Luke 11.14-28 & baptised 2 of Jacob Bates
daughters
Sunday the 13 P at st Johns Ch from the gospel John 6.
1-15 & on Monday the 14 P the funeral for John Bright
from the 24 Ps & on Thursday the 10 of March Married

Page 96: David Wilson to Bity Chupp
Thursday the 17 Married George Michael Koon to Christena Koon
Sunday the 20 P at Zion Ch from the gospel John 8.46-59
Thursday the 24 Married Martin Sox to Leah Lybrand
Sunday the 27 P at Salem H. C. from the Epistle Phil
2.5-11 & baptised one child

Thursday the 31 P a preparitorySermon from 1 Cor 11.28
& Confirmed 11 Persons & on Goodfriday the Rev. Houk &
myself P at Zion Church I P from Mat 26.26-28 & we administered the Sacrament to 106 Communicants.
Saturday the 2 of April P at St Peters Pineywoods from
1 Cor 11.28 I Confirmed 23 & baptised 1 child & on Easter
Sunday Rev Houk & myself administered the Sacrament at
Bethlehem Broad River I P from John 6.53 & we administered the Sacrament to 23 Persons & I baptised one child
Sunday the 10 of April P at St Johns Ch from the Gospel
John 20.19-31

Page 97: & in the afternoon P at Adam Risters from the epistle
1 John 5.4-10
Saturday the 16 of April I P at St Peters from 1 Cor
11.28 & on Sunday the 17 Friend Kleckly & myself P I
P from St John 6.53 & administered the Sacrament to
36 Persons & Confirmed 2 Persons & Baptised 2 children
Sunday the 24 of April P at Longs Church Edgefield from
Rom 10.4 & in the afternoon I P at St Pauls Ch lower
hollow Creek from Math 11.28 & baptised 1 child
Sunday the 1 of May I P at Salem upper hollow Creek
from the gospel St John 16.5-15 & in the afternoon I
P at Peters Ch from James 1.21
Sunday the 8 of May I P. at St Johns Church from the
gospel St. John 16.23-33 & on Sunday the 15 I P. at
Zion Church from the epistle 1 Peter 4.7-11 & baptised
one child & on Monday the 16 Buried old Mrs Miller &
p from Rom 8.18
Saturday the 21 of May P at St Johns from 116 Ps & 12.
13.14 verses & on Whitsunday friend Kleckly & myself P
he from Acts 16.30-31 & I P from the gospel John 14.23-31 & administered the Sacrament to 80 Communicants.

Page 98: On Friday the 3 of June 1836 Buried Jesse Lykes & P
from John 11.26 & on Sunday the 5 P at St Peters piney
woods from the Gospel Luke 16.19-31 & baptised 2 children
Sunday the 12 P at St Johns from Mat 11.28 & baptised
one child
Saturday the 18 of June P at Bethlehem Ch from Rom 8.1

Sunday the 19 P at Zion Ch from the gospel Luke 15.1-15 & baptised one child & in the afternoon P at St Peters Peters from Rom 8.1 & baptised one child
Sunday the 26 of June I P at Longs Ch from 1 Cor 1.30 & baptised 3 children & in the afternoon I P at St Pauls Ch from 1 Cor 3.11 & baptised one child
Sunday the 3 of July P at St Peters Piney woods from the gospel Luke 5.1-11 & baptised 4 children
Sunday the 10 of July P at St Johns Ch from the gospel Mat 5.20 & baptised one child
Sunday the 17 P at Zion Ch from the Epistle Rom 6.19-23 & baptised 3 children
I P at Bethlehem B River from 1 John 1.7
Sunday the 24 P at Salem Ch from the epistle Rom 8.12-17 & baptised 2 children & in the afternoon Buried Daniel Lomonick aged 85 & P from John 11.25-26
Sunday the 31 P at Peters from the

Page 99: Gospel Luke 16.1-9
Thursday the 4 of August P at thanksgiving Sermon in Zion Ch from the 92 Ps & 1 verse
Sunday the 7 of August P at St Peters Pineywoods from the Epistle 1 Cor 12.1-11 & baptised one child
Thursday the 11 of August Married Jacob Geiger to Selena Huffman
Sunday the 14 P at St Johns Ch from the epistle 1 Cor 15.1-10
Thursday the 18 Married Henry Kleckly to Winford E. Slone
Saturday the 20 P at Bethlehem from 2 Cor 3.6 & in the afternoon buried old Mr. Slice & P from John 5.24
On Sunday the 21 of August P at Zion Ch from the gospel Mark 7.31-37 & in the afternoon P at St. Peters from John 3.16 & baptised 4 children
Sunday the 28 P at Longs Ch from the gospel Luke 10. 23-37 & in the afternoon P at St. Pauls Ch from Gal. 3. 22 & on Monday gave Mrs. Hohheimer the Sacrament & on Tuesday the 30 Buried Lorence Roof & P from John 5.24
Friday the 2 of Septr Buried Robert Harris [?] daughter & P from John 5.24
Sunday the 4 P at St. ___

Page 100: from the epistle Gal. 5.16-24 & baptised one child
Wednesday the & Burried old Mr. Bouknight & P from Mat 25.46
Sunday the 11 P at St Johns Ch from the gospel Mat 6. 24-34 & baptised 2 children
Thursday the 15 Buried Noah Halmans child & P from John 5.24 & in the afternoon Married Nathanial Kleckly to Sarah Corley
Sunday the 18 P at Zion Ch from the epistle Ephes 3.13-21 & in the afternoon I P at St. Peters Ch from 1 Cor 1.21 & baptised 3 children
On Saturday & Sunday the 24 & 25 of Septr Bendenbaugh & myself P at Salem Ch I P on Sunday from Luke 22.19 & administered the Sacrament to about 80 & baptised 5 children & in the afternoon P at St. Pauls Ch from Mat 5.4.
Sunday the 2 of October P at St. Peters from the gospel Mat 22.14-46 & baptised 2 children & in the afternoon P the funeral for Nicholas Slights wife from Mat 24.44
Wednesday the 5 Buried Abraham Freys daughter & P from Heb 4.9 & on Saturday 8 P the funeral for John Elisers

son & P from 1 Cor 15.55 & on Sunday the 9 P at St. Johns Ch from the Gospel Mat 9.1-8 & baptised one child Thursday the 13 of October Ma-ried Joseph Gable to Mary Nipper

Page 101: Sunday the 16 of October I P at Zion Church from the Gospel Mat 22.14 & baptised one child & Married Daniel Wingard to Elisabeth Hook & in the afternoon P at St. Peters from Rom 1.16
Thursday the 20 Buried George Roberts Daughter & P from Luke 8.52
October Sunday the 23 1836 P at Longs Church & administered the Sacrament to 19 Communicants
Sunday the 30 of October I treated on the reformation at Bethlehem Church & baptised 2 children & in the afternoon P the funeral for old Mrs. Koon & her grand son & P from Heb 4.3
Sunday the 6 of Novr P at St. Peters Piney woods from the epistle Phil 3.17-21 & baptised one child
Thursday the 10 of Novr Married Daniel Koon to Eve Margaret Earigle
Sunday the 13 Burried Martin Hook Esqr & P from Heb 4.3. Synod
Sunday the 20 Rain
Tuesday the 22 Buried Gasper Amicks wife & P from Heb 4.3.
Sunday the 27 P at Salem Ch from the gospel Mat 21.1-9 & baptised 2 children & in the afternoon P in St. Pauls from Mark 1.15

Page 102: Sunday the 4 of December 1836 I P at St. Peters Piney woods from Mark 1.15 & baptised 1 child
Sunday the 11 P at St Johns from the gospel Mat 11.2-10 & baptised 3 children & in the afternoon I P at St Jacobs Ch from John 6.28.29
Saturday the 17 I P at Bethlehem Ch from Mark 1.15 & baptised one child & on Sunday the 18 P in Zion from the gospel John 1.19-28 & baptised one child & in the afternoon P in Peters from Mark 1.15 & baptised one child.
Christmas day Sunday the 25 P at Longs Church from the Gospel Luke 2.1-14 & on Monday I P at Salem Ch from Titus 2.14 & baptised 3 adults & 2 children Thursday 29 Married William Shull to Sharlet Roof & baptised 2 children
Sunday the 1 of January 1837 I P at Pineywood church from the gospel Luke 2.21-34 & baptised 3 children
Thursday the 5 Married John George Slice to Mary Ann Amick & on Epiphany I P at St Jacobs from the Gospel Mat 2.1-12
Sunday the 8 P at St Johns Ch from the epistle Rom 12.1-6 & baptised 2 children & in the afternoon I P the funeral for Adam Eptings Child from Heb 4.9
Tuesday the 10 Buried David Cromer

Page 103: & P from Rev 13.14 & on Saturday the 14 P the funeral for Abraham Boland from Rev. 14.13 & on Sunday in Zion Ch from the epistle Rom 12.6-16 & in the afternoon P in St Peters Ch from John 1.10
Thursday the 19 & Burried old Mrs Hokeheimer & P from a Text of her own choice 2 Tim 4.7.8.
Sunday the 22 I Preached at Salem Ch from the Gospel

Mat 20.1-16 & baptised 4 children
Sunday the 5 of February 1837 P at St. Peters piney
woods from the Gospel Luke 18.31-43 & baptised 1 child
& in the afternoon married Joshua Tayler to Catharine
Margaret Earigle
Tuesday 7 baptised Joshua Wingards Son.
Thursday the 9 Married Jacob Sox to Susanna Gable
Sunday the 12 P at St Johns Ch from the gospel Mat
4.1-11 & baptised 3 children & in the afternoon P
in St Jacobs Church from the gospel Mat 4.1-11 &
baptised one child
Sunday the 19 P at Zion Ch from the gospel Mat 15.21-
28 & baptised one child & in the afternoon I P at St.
Peters Ch from Mat 9.2
Thursday the 23 of Febry Married David Earigle to Mary
Magdalen Wessinger & in the afternoon Married Adam
Boland to Ann HIp
Sunday the 26 P at Salem Ch from the gospel Luke 11.
14-28 & baptised 4 children & Tuesday the 28 Married
John Price to Nancy Craps
Sunday the 12 of March 1837 P at St Johns from the
gospel John 8.47 & in the afternoon in St Jacobs from
the same & on Sunday the 19 I P in Zion Ch

(on a page between 102 and 103 are several scripture
passages copied and pasted in the book)

Page 104: from the Epistle 1 Cor 11.23-32 & in the after noon
I P in Peters ch from John 8.47 & on Thursday the 23
of March I Married David Miller to Sally Loreman.
Goodfriday I P in Zion from 2 Cor 5.21 & administered
the Sacrament 98 Com & Confirmed 5 Persons & baptised
one child on Saturday I P at Salem Ch from 1 Cor 11.28
& baptised 2 children & on Easter Sunday I P in Salem
Ch from Col 3.1 & Confirmed 39 persons & 138 Commnts.
Tuesday 28 Buried Mrs. Lybrand & P from Col. 3.4.
Saturday the 1 of April 1837 P at St. Peters piney woods
from 2 Cor 13.5 & Sunday the 2 of April I P from the
gospel John 20.19-31 & administered the Sacrament to
100 Communicants & baptised one child & on Tuesday the
4 Buried George Wingards wife Nancy & P from Rom 6.5.
Sunday the 9 of April the Rev. Adam Miller P for me
in St. Johns Ch & I baptised one child. He also P
for me in Zion church on the 16. & I baptised one
child
Sunday the 23 I P in Salem church from the epistle
James 1. 16-21 & in the afternoon I in St. Pauls Ch
from Gal. 3.10
Sunday the 30 P in St Peters or Meetzes from Rom 10.4
Ascensions Day May the 4 I P in Bethlehem ch from the
gospel Mark the 16. & baptised one child & on Friday
the 5 of May I P the Funeral for old Jacob Earigle

Page 105: & P from Gen 3.19
Sunday the 7 of May I P in St Peters Ch from Gal.
3.26.27 & baptised one child
Saturday the 13 of May I P in St Johns from Mark 1.15
& on Whitsunday I P from 1 cor 10.15.16 & administered
the Sacrament to   Commts & on Sunday being Whitond
 (sic) from the gospel St John 3.16-21 & on Sunday 21
I P in Zion from the Gospel St John 3.1-15 & baptised
3 children & in the afternoon I P in St. Peters from

St. John 3.7. Confirmed 2 Persons at St. Johns Ch
Sunday the 28 P in Salem Ch from the gospel Luke 16.
19-31 & baptised 3 children & in the afternoon P at
St. Pauls ch from 1 Peters 3.12
Sunday the 4 of June 1837 I P in Bethlehem ch from the
Gospel Luke 14 & baptised one child
Sunday the 11 The Rev. Abel John Brown P for me in St.
Johns Ch & I baptised one child
Sunday the 18 The Rev. Brown P for me in Zion ch & on
Thursday the 22 I P the funeral for Saml Wingards Wife
from Heb 4.9
Sunday the 25 the Rev. Brown P for me at Salem ch & I
baptised 2 children & Thursday the 29 of June 1837
Married Henry Earigle to Nancy Roll
Sunday the 2 of July I P in St Peters from the epistle
Rom 6.3-11 & baptised 4 children
Sunday the 9 of July 1837 in St Johns Ch from the Epi-
stle Ro. 6.19-23 & in the after noon I P at St. Jacobs
Ch from the epistle Rom 6.19-23 & baptised 2 children
Sunday the 16 of July I P in Zion Ch from the epistle
Rom 8.12-17 & baptised one child & in the afternoon

Page 106: I P in St. Peters ch from the 2 Cor 3.6.
Sunday the 23 of July I P in Salem Ch from the Epistle
1 Cor 10.6-13 & baptised 2 children
Sunday 30 P at Bethlehem Ch from the epistle 1 Cor 12.
1-11 & baptised one child
The first Sunday in August I P in St Peters Ch from
the Gospel Luke 18.9-14 & baptised one child
The second Sunday in August I P in St Johns Ch from
Gal. 5.17 & in the afternoon from the same text in
St Jacobs Ch & on Friday the 18 I P the funeral for
David Youngiers child from John 14.2 & on the third
Sunday I P in Zion Ch from the Gospel Luke 10.23-27
& baptised 2 children
Monday the 21 of August Buried Mapirs son & P from
Rom 3.23
The fourth Sunday in August I P in Salem Ch from the
Epistle Gal. 5.17 & baptised 3 children & in the af-
ternoon I P in St. Pauls from Rom 3.23
Septr Sunday the 10 P at St Johns from the epistle
Ephes 3.13-21 & baptised 1 child & in the afternoon
I P in St Jacobs ch from Gal. 1.4 & baptised 4
children
On the first Sunday in Septr I P in St Peters ch from
1 Cor 2.2 & baptised 6 children
Tuesday the 12 Burried one of David Younginers children
& P from 1 Thes 5.9
The third Sunday in Septr I P in Bethlehem church
from the epistle Ephes 4.1-6 & Sunday the 4 I P in
Salem Church from the gospel Mat 22.34-46 & baptised
3 children & in the afternoon I P in St. Pauls ch from
Gal. 1.4 & baptised one child

Page Tuesday 26 I P the funeral for one of Ruben Lybrands
children on Edisto from Col 3.4.
the first Sunday in October 1837 I P in St Peters' from
the Gospel Mat 9.1-8 & baptised 5 children & on Monday
the 2 I P the funeral for Thos Bookmans son from Col.
3.4.
Saturday the 14 I P the funeral for Peter Ramecks Wife
& P from Col. 3.4. & on Sunday the 15 of October P In
Zion Ch from the Gospel John 4.46-54 & in the after

noon I P in St Peters Ch from John 4.50 & baptised 4 children
Sunday the 22 I P in Salem Ch from the Epistle Phil 1.3-11 & baptised 2 children & in the afternoon I P in St. Pauls Ch from John 4.50
Monday the 23 I P the funeral for Emmanuel Seastrunk from 1 Peter 1.24 & baptised one child
Sunday 29 P at Bethlehem from Phil 3.21
Sunday the 5 of Novr 1837 P in St Peters from the Gospel Mat 9.18-26
Thursday the 9 Married Joseph Weed to Martha Stack
Sunday the 12 P in St Johns from Rom 3.20 & in the afternoon P in St Jacobs from Rom 5.1 & baptised one child
Tuesday the 14 Married Henry Miller to Polly Bowers.
Sunday the 19 I P in Zion Ch from the gospel Mat 25.31-46 & baptised one child & in the afternoon I P in St. Peters from Rom 10.10
Sunday 26 P at Salem Ch from the gospel Mat 24,25 & in the afternoon I P in St Pauls from Rom 10.10
The first Sunday in Decr 1837 P in St Peters from the gospel Mat 21.1-9 & baptised one child
Thursday the 7 Married Levi Sheley to Mary Barbara Earigle

Page 108: Sunday morning the 10 of Decr 1837 Married John Whites to Mary Shealey I then went & preached in St. Johns Ch from the gospel Luke 21.25-36 & in the afternoon I p in St. Jacobs Ch from Rom 10.10
Sunday the 17 of P in Zion Ch from Rom 10.10 & baptised 2 children
Sunday the 25 prevented from attending on account of rain, sleet & high water
Christmas I P in Zion Ch from the gospel Luke 2.1-14 & baptised one child
Wednesday the 27 Buried Thomas son of Peter Metz & P from Ps 8.4.
Sunday after Christmas P at Bethlehem from Gal. 4.1-7 & baptised 2 children
Epiphany I P in Meetzes Ch from the gospel Mat 2.1-12 & baptised 1 child & on the first Sunday in January 1838 I P in St Peters Ch from the epistle Rom 12.2 & baptised 2 children. The second Sunday in January I P in St Johns from the gospel John 2.1-11 & baptised one child & in the afternoon I P in St Jacobs from the gospel also the Saturday before I P the funeral for Jacob Erigles daughter from Heb 9.27
Thursday the 18 Married Michael Corley to Mary Turnipseed & baptised 2 children. The Third Sunday prevented on account of snow.

Page 109: Thursday the 25 of January 1838 Married James Jumper to Sarah Leaphart.
The fourth Sunday I P in Salem from the gospel Mat 8.23-27 & baptised 2 children & in the afternoon I P in St Pauls from the gospel Mat 8.23-27 & baptised one child & Thursday the 8 of February Married Jesse Coogler to Sparta Metz
The Second Sunday in Febry I P in St Johns from the gospel Mat 20.1-16 & baptised one child & in the afternoon in St Jacobs from the gospel & baptised one child

The Third Sunday I P in Zion Ch from the gospel Luke 8.4-15 & baptised one child
The Fourth Sunday I P in St. Peters or pineywoods from the gospel Luke 18.31-43
Friday the 2 of March attended the Convention of Inventions & Traditions of men
Tuesday the 6 of March Baptised young Christian Weeds child
Sunday the 11 of March the Rev. Mr. Brown P for me in St. Johns & I baptised 2 children
Tuesday the 13 I buried Christian Weeds Child & the Rev. Mr. Brown preached
Sunday the 18 I P in Zion Ch from the Gospel Luke 11. 14-28 & in the afternoon in St Peters from the gospel.
Sunday the 25 I P in Salem Ch from the epistle Gal. 4.21-31 & baptised 2 children & in the afternoon I P in St. Pauls from Gal. 5.1 & baptised one child

Page 110: Sunday the 1 of April I P in St Peters or piney woods from the Gospel John 8.46-59 & baptised one child
Thursday the 5 of April Married John George Fulmer to Margaret Bowers & on the second Sunday P In St. Johns from Gal. 5.1 & in the afternoon I P in St. Jacobs Ch from Gal. 5.1
Thursday the 12 I P in Zion Church from 1 John 1. 8.9 & on Good Friday I P from Math 26.26-28 & Confirmed 8 Persons & there were 95 Communicants & baptised 2 children & on Saturday I P in Bethlehem ch from 1 John 1. 8.9 & on Easter Sunday I P from Mat 26.28 Confirmed 8 Persons & baptised one adult & there were 39 Communicants
Easter Monday I P. in St. Peters Ch from the epistle Acts 10.34.35
Thursday the 19 of April 1838 Married George Lindler to Admelia Bouknight
Saturday the 21 I P in Salem Ch from 1 John 1.8.9 & baptised one child & on Sunday the 22 I P from Mat. 26.26-28 Confirmed 2 Persons & administered the Sacrament to 104 Communicants & in the afternoon I P in St. Pauls from John 6.47 & baptised 2 children
Sunday the 29 I P in Bethlehem from John 10.11-16
Sunday the 6 of May 1838 I attended with the Rev. Mr. Miller in St Peters Ch where I baptised 4 children & from there we went to Edisto where I baptised one child
Sunday the 13 I P in St Johns Ch from the epistle James 1.16-21 & baptised 4 children & in the afternoon I P in St Jacobs from the epistle & baptised one child.

Page 111: Sunday the 20 of May I P in Zion Church from the epistle James 1.25 & baptised one child
Sunday the 27 I P in Salem Ch from John 8.31 & in the afternoon I P in St Pauls from the same
Wednesday the 30 I buried Mrs Stuck & P from Col 3.4.
Sunday the 3 of June being Whitsunday I P in St. Peters from the Gospel John 14.23-31 & in the afternoon I P the funeral for Danl Koons wife from John 11.25.26 & on Monday the 4 I P the funeral for Eve Margaret Stoutmier from John 14.3
Sunday the 10 of June I P in St Johns from the gospel John 3.5 & in the afternoon I P in St. Jacobs from the gospel John 3.5

Tuesday the 12 I P the funeral for Capt Long wife from
Col 3.4 & baptised 2 children
Sunday the 17 P in Zion Ch from Luke 14.6 & baptised
one child & in the afternoon I P in St. Peters from
the same text.
Thursday 21 Married Godfrey Stack to Polly Weed.
Sunday the 24 of June P at Salem Ch from the gospel
Luke 14.16-24 & baptised Levi Halman's Wife & in
the afternoon P in St. Pauls Ch from the gospel
Sunday the 1 of July 1838 P in St. Peters from the
Gospel Luke 15.1-10 & baptised one child
Sunday the 8 P in St. Johns from 1 John 5.11 & baptised one child & in the afternoon I P in St. Jacobs
from the same text
Thursday 19 Burried Andrew Summer & P from 1 Thes 5.9

Page 112: Sunday 15 P in Zion from the Gospel Luke 5.1-11 &
in the afternoon I P from 1 Peter 3.12 in St. Peters
Sunday the 22 of July P in Salem from the gospel Mat
5.20-26 & baptised 4 children & in the afternoon I
P in St. Pauls from 1 Peter 3.12
Monday the 23 the Debate was held between Miller &
Hope
Sunday 29 Mr. Brown P for me in Bethlehem Ch from
Rom 3.23-24 & I baptised one child & in the afternoon
I baptised Joseph Weeds child
Sunday the 5 Rev. Brown P in St. Peters, or piney woods
Sunday the 12   do   P in St. Johns & in the afternoon he preached in St. Jacobs & I baptised 4
children on Monday he preached in Bethlehem
Sunday the 19 I P at Edisto & Mr Brown P in Zion &
St Peters, Sunday 26 Brown P for me in Salem Ch & I
baptised 3 children & in the afternoon he P for me in
in St. Pauls & on Monday 27 we preached in piney woods
I P from Thanksgiving Ps 118.1 & baptised 2 children
Sunday the 2 of Sept P in Piney wood Ch from the epistle
2 Cor 3.4-11 & baptised one child & on the second Sunday
in Sept I P in St. Johns from the epistle Gal. 3.15-22
& in the afternoon I P in St. Jacobs from the same.
Wednesday the 12 Buried Barefield that lived with Thos
Bookman & P from 1 Thes 5.9
Saturday 15 Buried old Saml Bookman & P from Ps 12.1.
The Third Sunday in Septr I P in Zion from the epistle
Gal. 5.17 & in the afternoon I P in St. Peters from ___
& baptised 2 children

Page 113: Thursday 20 Married William Wilson to Sarah Chupps &
baptised one child
The 4 Sunday in Septr I P in Salem Ch from Col 2.6. &
in the afternoon I P from the same in St. Pauls &
baptised one child
Sunday the 30 I P in Bethlehem Ch from Col 2.6.
October the 4 I P the funeral for George Slises child
from Mat 19.14 & on Saturday the 6 of October 1838
I P in St Peters or pineywoods Ch from 1 Cor 11.28 &
Confirmed 21 & baptised 3 children & on Sunday the 7
I P from 1 Cor 10.15.16 & administered the Sacrament
to 97 Comt
Sunday the 14 I P in St. Johns from the Gospel Luke
22.34 & baptised one child & in the afternoon I in St.
Jacobs from Rom 3.20
The Third sunday in October I P in Zion from the gospel

Mat 9.1- & in the afternoon I P in St. Peters from
Mat 9.2 & baptised one child
The fourth Sunday I P in St. Pauls little hollow creek
from 1 Cor 10.15 & on the day before I P from 1 Cor
11.28 & there were 34 Communicants & in the afternoon
on Sunday I P in Salem Ch from the gospel Mat 20.1-14
& baptised one child
Thursday the 1 of Novr 1838 I Married John George
Shely to Catharine Boland.
The first Sunday in Nov I P in Edisto Ch from the
gospel John 4.47-54
The Second Sunday in Nov I P in St. Johns from Mat
9.13
Saturday the 17 I P in Bethlehem Ch from Luke 7.59
The third Sunday in

Page 114:
Novr I P in Zion Ch from Luke 9.59
The fourth Sunday I P Salem from the gospel Mat 9.18-26
& baptised 3 children & in the afternoon I P in St.
Pauls from Luke 7.59
The first Sunday in Decr I P in St. Peters Piney woods
from the gospel Mat 21.1-9 & baptised 3 children
The second Sunday in Decr I P in St. Johns from Rom
1.16 & in the afternoon in St. Jacobs from the same &
baptised 4 children & in the afternoon in St. Peters
from the same
Thursday the 20 of Decr 1838 Married Joseph W. Oswald
to Pamelia Wick & on Sunday the 23 I P in Salem from
the gospel John 1.19-28 & baptised 3 children & in the
afternoon I P from the same in St. Pauls & On Christmas
day I P in Bethlehem from the gospel Luke 2. & on
Second Christmas day I P in St Jacobs from the gospel
Luke 2.15-29 $17 Sunday the 30 I P in Peters from the
epistle Gal. 4.1-7
Saturday the 29 I P the funeral for Caty Gibson daughter of John Elliser & P from Heb 4.3
The first Sunday in January 1839 I P in St Peters
piney woods from the gospel Mat 2.1-12 & baptised one
child $47
The second Sunday in Jany I P in St. Johns from the
epistle Rom 12.1-6 & baptised 2 children $43-25 & in
the afternoon in St. Jacobs from the same & baptised
one child
The third Sunday in January I P in Zion from the
epistle Rom 12.6-16 $16 & in the afternoon at St.
Peters from the same

Page 115:
Tuesday the 22 of January 1839 I P the funeral for
the Daughter of Andrew Summer from Heb 4.3. & on
Wednesday the 23 I P the funeral for Adaline Kelly
the daughter of George Kelly from Heb 4.3 & on Thursday the 24 I P the funeral for the widow Miller & P
from 1 Cor 15.55 $3
Friday the 25 I gave the Sacrament to Ben Roofs sis-
ter & commenced Catechism at Zion's Church
The fourth Sunday I P in Salem ch from the gospel
Mat 20.1-16 & baptised 2 children $30.50 & in the af-
ternoon I P in St. Pauls from the same $13.50
Saturday the 2 of Febry 1839 I P in St. Peters from
the gospel Luke 8. 4-15 & baptised 2 children $5
Febry the 5 Married David Koon to Caroline Chapman
$2 The second Sunday in Febry P in St. Johns from

the gospel Luke 18.31-43 & baptised one child. $11
Thursday the 14 Married Jacob Slise to Anna Magdalen
Ryster & baptised four children. The Third Sunday
I P in Zion from the gospel Mat 4.1-11 & baptised
one child $1.50 & in the afternoon I P from the same
in St. Peters & baptised 2 children
Thursday 21 Buried old Mrs. Sease & P from Heb 4.3 $1
The fourth Sunday in Febry I P in Salem Ch from the
gospel Mat 15.21-28 & baptised 2 children $2 & in the
afternoon I P in St. Pauls from the Same
Tuesday the 26 I Married Drury J. Harman to Charlotte
Rall $5.

Page 116: Thursday the 28 of Febry 1839 Married Benj Roof to
Charlotte Shull $1
The first Sunday in March the Rev. Mr. Brown P for me
in St. Peters or piney woods Church $5 & I baptised
one child & in the afternoon Mr Brown P at Henry Dom-
inicks & I baptised 5 children. $2
The second Sunday in March I P in St. Johns from the
gospel St. John 5.1-16 & baptised 3 children $8 & in
the afternoon I P in St. Jacobs Ch from the same &
baptised one child $8
The first Saturday in March the Rev. Mr. Brown preached
for me in Bethlehem on Broad River & I baptised 3 children
The fourth Sunday in March I P in Salem Ch from Phil
3.9 & baptised one child & in the afternoon from the
same in St. Pauls & baptised one child
Monday the 25 of March I P the funeral for Barbara
Roof from 1 Cor 15.55
Thursday the 28 I P in Peters Church from 1 Cor 11.28
& Confirmed 8 Persons & on Goodfriday I P from 1 Cor
10.15.16 & administered the Sacrament to 30 Communicants
Saturday the 30 I P in Zion Church from 1 Cor 11.28 &
Confirmed 6 & on Easter Sunday I P from 1 Cor 10. 15.
16 & administered the Sacrament to 106 Communicants &
baptised 2 children & on Easter Monday I P in Bethlehem from Rom 4.25
The first Sunday in April 1839 I P in St. Peters piney
woods from the gospel St. John 20.19-31.

Page 117: The Second Sunday in April 1839 I P in St. Johns from
the Gospel St. John 10.11-16 & baptised 3 children &
in the afternoon I P from the same at St. Jacobs &
baptised 2 children
Wednesday the 17 of April I P the funeral for old Mrs.
Meetze & P from the 90 Ps 10.12 verses.
The Third Sunday in April I P in Bethlehem from 1 Cor
10.15.16 & administered the Sacrament to 41 Communicants
& baptised one child & on the Saturday before I P from
1 Cor 11.28 & confirmed 6 Persons.
The 4 Sunday in April I P in Salem Ch from the gospel
John 15.5-15 & baptised 4 children & in the afternoon
I P from the same & baptised one child
Thursday the 2 of May 1839 Married Azariah Crout to
Ghristena Lybrand
The first Sunday in May I P in St. Peters pineywoods
from the gospel John 16.23-30 & baptised one child &
in the afternoon P from the same in St. Peters Ch
on Monday the 13 I P the funeral for George Wheeler

from 1 Thes 5.9
Saturday the 18 I P in Salem Ch from Heb 4.1 & baptised 2 Adults & one child & On Sunday the 19 being Whit Sunday I P from 1 Cor 11.26 & confirmed 5 Persons & administered the Sacrament to 97 Comts & in the afternoon I P in St. Pauls from the gospel John 14.23
Whitsunmonday I P in Bethlehem Ch from the gospel John 3.16-21 & baptised one child
Tuesday the 21 of May P the funeral for William Malur's child from Rev. 14.13
Thursday the 23 of May Married Jessee Drafts to Nancy Lorick.

Page 118: The fourth Sunday being Trinity Sunday I P in St. Johns Ch from the gospel John 3.1-15 & baptised 2 children & in the afternoon I P from the same in St. Jacobs & baptised one child.
The first Sunday in June I P in St. Peters or piney woods from the gospel Luke the 16.19-31
Tuesday the 4 of June I buried Adam Epting & P from Luke 12.40 & on Wednesday the 5 I buried John Craps child & P from Rev. 14.13
The second Sunday in June I P the funeral for William Chapman from Ps 12.1 & baptised 2 children & in the after noon I P in St. Jacobs from the gospel Luke 14.16-24 & baptised one child.
Thursday the 13 of June Buried Andrew Cromer & P from Ps 12.1
The Third Sunday in June I P in Zion Ch from the gospel Luke 15.1-10 & in the afternoon in St. Peters from the same
The fourth Sunday I P in Salem from Rom 8.7 & baptised 2 children & one adult & in the afternoon I P st. Pauls from the same
Wednesday the 26 of June I Buried old Mrs. Roof & P from Col 3.3
Saturday the 29 I P in Zion Ch from Acts 14.17 a Thanks giving sermon the 5 Sunday I P Bethlehem from the Epistle 1 Peter 3.12 & baptised 2 children.
The first Sunday in July I P in St. Peters or piney woods from the gospel Mat 5.20 & baptised 4 children & in

Page 119: the afternoon I P the funeral for old Mrs. Metz from Col 3.3 The Second Sunday in July I P in St. Johns from the epistle Rom 6.19-23 & in the afternoon I P the funeral for Gerard Wiggars child from John 14.3
The third Sunday in July I P in Zion Ch the funeral sermon for John Batys child from Ps 34.19 & baptised 3 children & in the afternoon in St. Peters from Rom 10.4
On the Saturday before the second Sunday in July I P at thanksgiving Sermon in Bethlehem Ch from Acts 14.17. On Thursday the 25 of July I Married Henry Hillard Sea to Catharine Snyder
The Fourth Sunday in July I P in Salem Ch from the gospel Luke 16.1-9 & baptised 5 children & one adult & in the afternoon I Buried Adam Shulls child & P from John 14.3
The first Sunday in August I P in Piney woods Ch from the gospel Luke 19.41-48 & baptised 2 children
Saturday the 10 of August 1839 I P in Bethlehem Ch from Luke 18.9-14 & on the second Sunday in August

I P in St. Johns from the gospel Luke 18.9-14 & in
the afternoon from the same in St. Jacobs & Baptised
2 children
The third Sunday I P Zion Church from the epistle 2
Cor 3.4-11 & baptised 2 children & in the afternoon I
P from the same in St. Peters Church
The Third Sunday or 18 day in August 1839 I Married
John Wingard to Mary Kleckly
The fourth Sunday in August P in Salem from the gospel
Luke 10.25-37 & in the afternoon in St. Paul from the
same Efies child born the 25 of August 1839
The first Sunday in Sept 1839 I P in St. Peters Ch
from the epistle Gal. 5.16-24 & baptised 3 children.
Friday the 6 of Septr I Buried old Mrs Price & P from
John14.2.3 & on the second Sunday in Septr I P in St
Johns from

Page 120: the gospel Mat 6.25-34 & baptised 2 children & in the
afternoon I P in St. Jacobs from the same & baptised
2 children & on Monday morning I baptised Henry
Metzs son Jacob Albert
The Third Sunday in Septr I P in Zion Ch from Mark
1.15 & baptised 3 children & in the afternoon I P
in St. Peters from the same
Thursday the 19 of Septr 1839 buried Mrs. Brassell & P
from 1 Thes 5.9
The fourth Sunday in Septr I P in Salem Ch from the
epistle Ephes 4.1-6 & baptised one child & in the
afternoon from the same & baptised one child
Thursday the 3 of October 1839 buried one of Jacob
Mayers sons & P from 1 Peter 1.22-25 & the first Sun-
day in October I P in St. Peters piney woods from the
epistle Ephes 4. 22-28 & baptised 2 children.
Saturday the 12 of October I P in Bethlehem from Mat 22.
34-40
The second Sunday I P in St. Johns from the same & in
the afternoon I P in St. Jacobs from the same
Thursday the 10 Buried one of Joseph Earharts Daughters
& P from 1 Peter 1.22-25
Thursday the 17 of October 1839 Married John Lorick to
Mary Ann Huffman
The third Sunday in October I P in Zion Ch from the
gospel St. John 4.47-54 & in the afternoon from the
same in St. Peters
The fourth Sunday in Salem from the gospel Mat 18.23-
35 & in the afternoon in lower hollowcreek Ch from
the Same
Thursday the 31 of October 1839 Married David Holman
to Anna Sease & baptised one child
The first Sunday in Novr P in piney woods Ch from the
epistle Phil 3.17-21
The second Sunday in Novr I P in St. Johns from Col
1.28 & baptised one child & in the afternoon in St.
Jacobs from Col 1.22 & on Wednesday P the funeral
for George Comalanders child from Luke 8.52

Page 121: [baptised] one child.
Thursday the 14 of Novr 1839 Married Samuel Corley
to Fanney Boney.
The Third Sunday in Novr Jacob Kleckley P for me in
Zion Ch & I baptised 2 children.

Monday the 18 Burried George Bouknights son & P from
1 Thes 4.13
Saturday the 23 P in Salem Ch from 1 Cor 15 & was
prevented from preaching on account of rain
Saturday the 30 of Novr I P the funeral for Simion
Wheelers child & P from John 8.51
The first Sunday in Decr 1839 I P in St. Peter piney
woods from Heb 6.18 & baptised 4 children
Thursday the 5 of Decr Married Jeremiah Miller to
Sally Earigle
The second Sunday in Decr I P the funeral for Jacob
Slices child from Gen 3.19 & P in St. Johns Ch from
Rom 15.13 & baptised 2 children & in the afternoon I
P in St. Jacobs Ch from the same
The third Sunday I P in Zion from Heb 6.18 & in the
afternoon from the same in St. Peters
Wednesday the 18 Buried Hilliard Sen's child & P from
1 Thes 4.13
The fourth Sunday prevented on account of snow & rain
Christmas I P in St. Jacobs from the gospel Luke 2.1-14
Thursday 26 Baptised 3 children at Cooglers
The Fifth Sunday in Decr The Rev. A. J. Brown preached
for me at Bethlehem & I Baptised 2 children
Monday the 30 Buried old Mr. Loner & Mr Brown preached.
The first Sunday in January 1840 Mr Brown P for me in
St. Peters pineywoods & I baptised 3 children & one
adult & in the afternoon we preached the funeral for
John Sultans child & on Monday we attended at Bethlehem Ch from the epistle
The second Sunday in Jany I P in Bethlehem Ch from the
epistle Rom 12.1-6 on Monday buried Joseph Bolands
child & Mr. Brown P
Thursday the 9 of Jany I P the funeral for Jeremiah
Wingard from Heb. 2.6. Thursday the 16 married Jacob
Senn[?] to Elisabeth Jane Frats. The third Sunday
P from Rom 8.1 & baptised

Page 122: 3 children
The fourth Sunday I P in Salem from ___ 8.1 & baptised
3 children. Thursday the 30 of January 1840 Married
Reuben Vinsant to Flora Price. The first Sunday in
Feby I P in Piney woods church from the gospel Mat
8.23-37 & baptised one child. Thursday the 6 of Febry
I buried Nancy Vinsant & P from 1 Thes 4.13.
The second Sunday I P in St. Johns from the Gospel
Mat 13. 24-30 & in the afternoon at St. Jacobs from
the same. The third Sunday in Febr Mr. Harris P for
me in Zion & I baptised 2 children & in the afternoon
I P in St. Peters from Col. 2.6 & baptised 1 child
Thursday the 20 buried one of Joseph Bolands children
& preached from Rom 8.18
The fourth Sunday in Feby I P in Salem Ch from the gospel Luke 8 & baptised one child & in the afternoon I
P in little hollowcreek Ch from Col 2.6. Monday the
24 of Feby buried Lewis George & P from John 14 & the
latter part of the 2 & 3 verses.
Thursday the 27 of Feby buried Azariah Crouts wife
& P from 2 Cor 5.1
The first Sunday in March 1840 I P in St. Peters piney
woods from the gospel Luke 18.31-43 & baptised 4 children on Monday I P in Salem Ch from Gal. 2.20
Saturday the 7 I P in Bethlehem from Gal. 2.20. The

second Sunday in March I P in St. Johns from the gospel Mat 4.1-11 & baptised 2 children & in the afternoon from the same in St. Jacobs Ch & baptised one child
Tuesday the 10 of March Married Andrew Shealy to Mary Caroline Sease. The third Sunday in March I P in Zion Ch from the gospel Mat 15.21-28 & baptised one child & in the afternoon I P in St. Peters from the same.

Page 123: Thursday the 19 I Married Michael Lindler to Kesiah Earigle
The Saturday before the fourth Sunday I P at Squer[sic] Addys from Mat 9.13 & on Sunday I P in Salem Ch from the gospel Luke 11.28 & baptised one child & in the afternoon I P in lower hollow creek Ch from St. Johns 8.31 & baptised one child
Tuesday the 24 of March 1840 I burried Daniel Wingards son & P from John 5.24.
Wednesday the 25 I buried Mary Stack & baptised 2 children.
The 5 Sunday in March I P in Bethlehem Ch from St. John 5.25.
Tuesday the 31 of March I buried old Mrs. Summers & preached from 2 Cor 5.4.
Thursday the 2 of April 1840 I Married James Hillard Calk to Mary Ann Elliser & baptised one child.
The first Sunday in April I P in St. Peters or piney woods from the gospel St. John 8.46-59 & baptised 3 children
Thursday the 9 of April 1840 I married Christian Price to Sally Oswalt
The second Sunday in April I P in St. Johns Ch from Rom 7.22 & baptised 2 children & in the afternoon I P from the same in St. Jacobs Ch
Goodfriday I P in Bethlehem on Broad River from Isa 53 & baptised one adult & on Saturday I P a preparatory sermon in Zion Ch from Prov. 16.1 & baptised one child. On Easter Sunday P from Mat 26.26-28 & administered the Sacrament to 111 Communicants & Confirmed one adult & baptised 3 children
The fourth Sunday in April 1840 I P in Salem Ch from the gospel John 20.19-31 & in the afternoon from the same in St. Pauls & baptised one child.
The first Sunday in May I P in St Peters or pineywoods from the gospel John 10.11-16 & baptised 2 children.
The second Sunday in May I P in St. Johns Ch from the gospel John 16.16-23 & baptised one child

Page 124: The second Sunday in May the 1840 I Married George Washington Bowers to Mary Magdalen Mayers
The 3 Sunday in May I P in Zion Ch from the epistle James 1.21 & in the afternoon I P in St. Peters from the same & baptised one child
The Saturday before fouth Sunday in May I P Salem Ch from 1 Cor 28 & baptised one adult & one child Confirmed 32 Persons & on Sunday I P from Mat 26. 26-28 & administered the Sacrament to 120 Communicants.
Ascension day I P in St. Jacobs Ch from the gospel Mark 16.14-20 & baptised one child The fifth Sunday in May I P in Bethlehem Ch from Mat 26.26-28 Confirmed 3 persons & administered the Sacrament to 35 Comts on the Saturday before I P from 1 Cor 11.28.
The first Sunday in June I P in St. Peters piney woods

from the gospel John 14.23-31 & baptised 2 children.
The second Sunday in June I P in St. Johns from the
gospel St. John 1.1-15 & baptised 3 children & in the
afternoon I P from the same in St. Jacobs & on Monday
I attended Lexington Court of Equity until Saturday
evening & on the Third Sunday I P in Zion from the
epistle 1 John 4.19 & in the afternoon from the same
in St. Peters
On the night of the 23 June I baptised Godfrey Stacks
son
Thursday the 25 of June I Married Joseph Fulmer to
Elisabeth Epting.
The fourth Sunday in June I P in Salem Ch from the
gospel Luke 14.16-24 & baptised 3 children & in the
afternonn I P from the same in St. Pauls little hollow
creek.
Wednesday the first of July I P the funeral for John
H. Sultans wife from 2 Peter 3.14.

Page 125:   ___ the 3 of July I P the funeral for John Baileys
child from 2 Peter 3.14.
The first Sunday in July I P in St. Peters from the
gospel Luke 15.1-10. The second Sunday I P in St.
Johns from Gal. 2.17 & baptised one child & P the
funeral for Easter Swittenberg from 1 Peter 1.24 & in
the afternoon I P in St. Jacobs from Gal. 2.17
The third Sunday in July I P in Zion from Luke 18.13
& baptised one child & in the afternoon I P from the
same in St. Peters & on the Saturday before I P in
Bethlehem from the same.
The fourth Sunday in July I P in Salem Ch from the
gospel Mat 5.20 & baptised 2 children & in the afternoon from the same in St. Paul & on Monday the 27 of
July I Buried Sebastian Younginger & P from Gen 3.19.
Thursday the 30 baptised Mrs. Youngingers son.
The first Sunday in August I P in St. Peters from the
epistle Rom 6.19-23
Wednesday 5 Buried Elijah Fullmer & preached from Gen.
3.19. The second Sunday I P in St. Johns from the
epistle Rom 8.12-17 & baptised one child & in the after-
noon I P from the same St. Jacobs Ch & baptised one
child.
Thursday the 13 of August 1840 Married Jesse Corley to
Abigial Rolen. The Third Sunday in August P in Zion
Church from St. John 6.68 & baptised one child & in
the afternoon from the same in St. Peters ch & baptised
one child.
The fourth Sunday in August P in Salem Church from 2
Tim 1.10 & in the afternoon from the same in lower
hollow creek church.
Monday the 24 of August I buried Godleab Sox & P from
2 Tim 1.10
Thursday 27 baptised Sanders Swigards son & at the same
time & baptised Wade Alexander, son of George Lorick
The fifth Sunday in August I baptised Lewis Stacks
daughter & P in Bethlehem from the epistle 1 Cor 15.1.2.
The first Sunday in Sept 1840 I P in St. Peters from the
epistle 2 Cor 3. & baptised 2 children & in the afternoon Buried Batys child & P from ___ 18.16 & on Wednesday the 9 I baptised Mathias Cooglers child.

Page 126: I preached in St. Johns on the second Sunday in Septr
from the gospel Luke 10.23-37 & also from the same in
the afternoon in St. Jacobs Church. The third Sunday
in Septr I P in Zion Ch from the epistle Gal. 5.16-24
& baptised one child & in the afternoon I P from the
same in St. Peters. The fourth Sunday in Sept 1840 I
P in Salem Ch from the gospel Mat 6.24-34 & baptised
4 children & in the afternoon preached from the same
in St. Paul. The first Sunday in October 1840 I P
in St. Peters from the gospel Luke 7.11-17 & baptised
3 children
The second Sunday I P in St John from the gospel Luke
14.1-11 & baptised 2 children & in the afternoon from
the same in St. Jacobs & baptised one child.
On Monday the 12 of October I P the funeral for John
Monts son from Luke 7.13-15.
Wednesday the 14 I Buried William Fraisher & P from 1
Cor 15.55-57.
The Third Sunday in October I P in Zion Ch from Phil
3.9 & baptised 2 children & in the afternoon I P in
St. Peters from the same on Monday the 19 I Buried
Jesse Tarrers son John Jacob & P from Job 14.1.2. &
baptised John Loricks daughter.
Saturday the 24 P the funeral for Andrew Tarrer & P
from Job 7.9.10.
The fourth Sunday in October I P in Salem Ch from the
gospel Mat 9.1-8 & baptised 3 children & in the
afternoon I P from the same in St. Pauls & on Friday
the 30 I buried Michael Drafts Daughter & P from Mark
10.13-16.
The first Sunday in Novr 1840 I P in St. Peters from the
gospel Mat 22.1-14 & baptised one child & on Monday I
Baptised Reuben Grosses child & on Tuesday the 3 of
Novr I Buried West Bickleys child & P from Job 7.9.10
The second Sunday in Novr I P in St. Johns from the
gospel John 4.47-54 & baptised one child & in the afternoon I P from the same in St. Jacobs

Page 127: _____ one child.
The third Sunday I P in Zion from the gospel Mat 18.
23-35 & baptised one child & Married John Inginer to
Elisabeth Gable & in the afternoon I P from the same
in St. Peters & baptised one child
Thursday the 26 of Novr 1840 I married John Francklow
to Julia Harman.
Sunday morning the 29 I Married Dr. Jacob K. Gant to
Prisilla Viel & then Preached in Bethlehem Ch from
1 Tim 1.15 & baptised one child.
The first Sunday in Decr 1840 I P in St. Peters from
1 Tim 1.15 & The Rev. Brown attended with me & I
baptised one child.
On the 2 Sunday the Rev. Brown preached for me in St.
Johns & in the afternoon he preached from St. Jacobs
& I baptised one child.
The 3 Sunday in Decr he preached for me in Zion & I
baptised one child & in the afternoon he preached in
St. Peters & on Tuesday evening he preached in the
Court House & on Thursday he married Christian Swigards
son to Addys daughter & I married Nicholas Washington
Groaner to Harriet Tarrer.
Friday Christmas Day Mr. Brown P for me in Bethlehem
Ch & on Saturday we attended at Fed Seases & administered the Sacrament to his wifes mother I P from Luke

22.19 on Sunday he preached for me in Salem Church & I baptised 8 children & in the afternoon he preached in little hollowcreek. The first Sunday in January 1841 I P piney woods or St. Peters from the gospel Mat 3.13-17. On Tuesday the 5 I buried old Mrs. Bickley & preached from Heb 13.14 & on Wednesday Old Christmas Day & preached in Salem from the gospel Mat 2.1-12. The second Sunday in January I P in St. Johns Ch from the gospel Luke 2 & in the afternoon in St. Jacobs Ch from the same.
Tuesday 19 I preached & administered the Sacrament to Mrs. Jackson & on Friday the 22 I P the funeral for Simon Addys child from Rev. 14.13 & Saturday I P the funeral

Page 128: Greens Child from Rev. 21.4 & on the fourth Sunday in January I P Salem Ch from Heb. 12.1.2. & in the afternoon I P in St. Pauls from the same & baptised children. Monday the 25 of January 1841 I buried old Mrs. Franklow & preached from Col. 3.4.
Saturday the 30 buried Mrs. Jackson & preached from Col. 3.4.. The 5 Sunday in January I P in Bethlehem Ch from Col. 3.4. The first Sunday in Febry 1831 I P Pineywoods Church from Heb. 12.1.2. & baptised 1 child Wednesday the 10 I buried Jesse Shealys son & P from Mark 10.14 & baptised one child.
The Third Sunday I P in Zion Ch from Luke 8.8. & baptised 2 children & in the afternoon preached in St. Peters from the same & baptised one child.
The 4 Sunday in Feby I P in Salem from the gospel Mat 4.1-8 & baptised one child & in the afternoon I P in St. Pauls from Mat 4.4. Wednesday the 3 of March 1841 preached the funeral for Mathias Slices child from Rev. 14.13
The first Sunday in March I P in St. Peters from the gospel Mat 15.21-28. The Second Sunday in March I P in St. John from the epistle Ephes 5.1-13 & baptised children & in the afternoon in St. Jacobs from the same & baptised 3 children.
Saturday the 13 of March buried Henry Amicks child & P from 2 Cor 5.1
The Third Sunday in March I P in Zion Ch from the Epistle Ephes 4.21-31 & in the afternoon from the same in St. Peters & baptised one child.
The fourth Sunday in Salem ch from the epistle Heb 9. 11-15 & baptised one child & in the afternoon from the same in St. Paul & baptised one child. On Goodfriday I P in Zion Ch from Isa 53.5.6 & in the afternoon from the same in St. Peters & baptised 2 children.
On Wednesday the 14 of April I buried Henry Haltawanger

Page 129: & preached from Heb. 9.27. The third Sunday in April 1841 I P in St. Pauls from the gospel John 20.29 & administered the Sacrament to 26 Comts & on Sautrday the day before I P from 1 John 1.8.9. & on Sunday afternoon I P in Salem Ch from John 20-31 & baptised one child. Sunday the 18 of April 1841 I married Eli Killian to Mary Ann Waddle.
The fourth Sunday in April I Preached in St. Johns from the epistle 1 Peter 2.25 & baptised 2 children & in the afternoon from the same in St. Jacobs & baptised one child.

The first Sunday in May 1841 I preached in St. Peters from the gospel John 16.16-23 & baptised 4 children & in the afternoon I P the funeral for Thomas Warners child from 1 Thes 4.13 on Tuesday the 4 I buried old Mrs. Rinehart & preached from 2 Tim 1.10. The third Sunday in May I P in Zion from 1 Cor 1.21 & in the afternoon from the same in St. Jacobs. On Ascension day I P in Bethlehem Ch from the gospel Mark 16.14-20 & baptised one child. The fourth Sunday I P in Salem Ch from John 16.13 Confirmed 2 & baptised 3 children & administered the Sacrament to 118.
The Saturday before I P from 1 John 1.8.9. On Sunday I P in little hollow creek & preached from John 16.7
Saturday the 29 of May 1841 I P the funeral for Emanuel Seastrunk from Job 14.1.2.
Whit Sunday I P in St. Jacobs Ch from the gospel John 14.23-31 & baptised 3 children
Whitsun Monday in Bethlehem Ch from the gospel St. John 3.16-21
Tuesday the 1 of June buried John Adam Miller & P from John 17.24
The first Sunday in June in St. Peter from the gospel St. John 3.1-15 The second Sunday in St. John & P from the

Page 130: epistle 1 John 4.16 & baptised 2 children & in the afternoon in St. Jacobs from the same & baptised one child. Saturday 19 of June P in Zion Ch from 1 John 1.8.9 & in the afternoon I buried Henry Shealy & p from Exxles 12.7. Sunday the 20 of June I P in Zion from the gospel Luke 14.16-24 Confirmed 8 & administered the Sacrament to 102 Communicants & baptised 2 children & one adult & in the afternoon I P from the same in St. Peters & baptised one child
The fourth Sunday in June Preached in Salem from the gospel Luke 15.1-10 & baptised 4 children & in the afternoon from the same in St. Pauls The first Sunday in July Preached from the epistle Rom 8.18-23.
Thursday the first day of July I Married William Stone to Mary Ann Kleckly. The second Sunday in July P in St. Johns from the epistle 1 Peter 3.8.15 & baptised one child & in the afternoon from the same in St. Jacobs & baptised one child. The third Sunday in July I P in Zion Ch from the gospel Mat 5.20. The fourth Sunday I P in Salem church from Mat 5.20 & baptised one child & in the afternoon in St. Pauls from the same & baptised one child.
The first Sunday in August I P in St. Peters from the epistle Rom 8.14 & baptised one child.
The second Sunday in August p in St. Johns from the gospel Luke 16.1-9 & baptised one child. In the afternoon prevented from preaching on account of rain. Saturday the 14 of August buried Philip Alewins child & P from Ecclesiastes 12.7. The third Sunday P in Zion C from Col 1.14 & in the afternoon from the same in St. Peters. Saturday the 21 of August I buried Nicholas Vinsant & P from Job 7.9.10. The fourth Sunday in August I P in Salem Ch from

Page 131: The epistle 1 Cor 15.1-10 & baptised one child & in the afternoon I Buried Jacob Holman Senr & p from 1 Cor 15.55.56.57 & baptised Daniel Oxoners child.

Saturday the 28 of August 1841. Preached a preparatory sermon in Bethlehem Ch from 1 John 1.8.9. & on Sunday I P from Heb 10.23 & administered the Sacrament to 24 Communicants.
On Wednesday the first of Septr I buried one of William Eptings children & preached from Job 7.9.10.
The first Sunday in Septr P in St. Peters from Heb. 10.23 & baptised one child. Tuesday the 7 of Septr burried Simion Wheelers child & preached from Luke 8.52. The second Sunday in Septr I P in St. John from Jude 3 & in the afternoon from the same in St. Jacobs. Tuesday 14 I buried David Chapmans daughter & preached from Luke 8.12. Wednesday the 15 of Septr 1841 buried Christian Swigard & P from St. John 5.24. The third Sunday I was prevented from attending my appointment on account of high water.
Monday the 20 I buried Uriah Wessingers son John & preached from Heb 13.14 & on Tuesday the 21 I buried Uriah Cooglers Wife & P from St. John 5.24.
The fourth Sunday in Sept I preached the funeral in Salem church for Joel Rices child from Luke 7.11-17 & in the afternoon I buried John Kinslers daughter & P from John 11.25 & baptised 3 children. On Friday the 1 of October I buried old Mrs. Riddle & preached from John 11.25.
The first Sunday in October I P in St. Peters from the Gospel Luke 14.1-11.
Wednesday the 6 of October I buried George Monts & preached from John 11.25 & baptised one child. The second Sunday I P in St John & in the afternoon in St. Jacobs & on Wednesday the 13 I buried

Page 132: David Millers child & preached from John 14.1.2. & baptised & Confirmed Mrs. Fulmer.
Thursday the 14 of Octr 1841 I buried Eli Freshlys child & P from John 11.25. The 3 Sunday in Octr P in Zion from the Epistle Eph 4.22-28 & baptised one child & in the afternoon P from the same in St. Peters. The fourth Sunday in Octr I P in Salem ch from the gospel Mat 22.1-14 & in the afternoon from the same in St. Pauls. Friday the 29 I P the funeral for Jacob Kynards Daughter from John 16.27. The fifth Sunday I P in Bethlehem a funeral sermon for Drury Davis son from John 16.27.
The first Sunday in November 1841 I P in Jacob Mayers house from the gospel Mat 18.23-35 & baptised 3 children. The second Sunday in Nov 1841 I P in St. Johns ch from Ephes 2.8-10 & baptised one child & in the afternoon from the same in St. Jacobs & baptised one child. The Third Sunday in Nov I P in Zion from Col 1.14 & in the afternoon from the same in St. Peters Thursday the 25 of Novr 1841 Married David Shull to Nancy Roof & baptised 2 children.
The fourth Sunday I was prevented on account of snow & sleet.
The first Sunday in Decr 1841 I P in Jacob Mayers House from the epistle Rom 15.4-13. The second Sunday in St. Johns from the gospel Mat 11.2-10 & in the afternoon from the same in St. Jacobs.

Page 133: The third Sunday in Zion Church from the gospel St. John 1.19-28. Thursday the 23 o Decr 1841 Married John Miller to Jemima Lorman.

Christmas day I P in Bethlehem Ch from the gospel.
The first Sunday in January 1842 I P at Jacob Mayers
from the gospel Mat 3.13-17 & baptised 3 children.
The second Sunday in Jany I P in St. Johns from the
epistle Rom 12.1-6 $28½ & in the afternoon in St.
Jacobs from the same $12½. The third Sunday in January
1842 I P in Zion from the gospel St. John 2.1-11 $17½
& in the afternoon from the same in St. Peters.
The fourth Sunday in January 1842 I Married David
Oswalt to Caroline Rall & Mr Brown P in Salem Church
$16.25 & in the afternoon he P in St. Pauls $10.37.
The fifth Sunday Mr. Brown P in Bethlehem $19
I baptised 6 children in Salem church & one in Bethlehem Church.
The first Sunday in Feby Mr Brown P in St. Peters Ch
& I baptised 4 children. The second Sunday in Feby
Mr Brown P for me in St. Johns & St. Jacob & on the
3 Sunday he preached for me in Zion & I baptised 2
children & on the last Wednesday in Feby I buried Mrs.
Evins & preached from Mat 25.13. The 4 Sunday I
preached in Salem from the epistle Eph 5.1-13 & in
the afternoon from the same in St. Pauls. Mr Brown
started home on the first day of March 1842.
Wednesday 2 of March I buried Henry Koon & Preached
from 2 Tim 1.10 & on Thursday the 3 of March I buried
Henry Shealy & P from 2 Tim 1.10.

Page 134: The first Sunday in March 1842 I preached at Jacob
Mayers from the epistle Gal. 4.21-31 & baptised 5
children.
Thursday the 10 I buried David Younginer & preached
from Mat 25.13.
Friday 11 buried old Mr Risinger & preached from Mat
25.13. The second Sunday in March I Preached in St.
Johns from the epistle Heb 9.11-15 & baptised one
child & in the afternoon I P in St. Jacobs from the
same & baptised 2 children & on Saturday I baptised
Hooks child.
Thursday the 17 I buried Polly Longs son & P from
1 Cor 15.12. The third Sunday I P in Bethlehem ch
from the epistle Phil 2.5-11 & baptised 2 children.
Thursday the 24 I P in Zion ch from Ps 139.23.24 &
baptised one child & on Goodfriday Mr. Rhodes preached
for me in Zion ch & we administered the Sacrament to
110 Communicants & Confirmed 5 persons.
Saturday the 26 Mr Rhodes P for me in Salem ch from
Mat 11.28-30 & on Easter Sunday we both preached I
P from Col. 3.1 Confirmed 5 & we administered the
Sacrament to 98.
The first Sunday in April 1842 Mr Rhodes preached from
Mark 1.15 & I baptised 2 children. Thursday the 7
I buried Ulrick Mayers Wife & P from 1 Cor 15.19.
The 2 Sunday in April Mr Rhodes preached for me in St.
Johns & I baptised one child & in the afternoon I bap-
tised one child in St. Jacobs church.

Page 135: Tuesday the 12 of April 1842 Married Joel George to
Polly Bright. The Third Sunday in April Mr. Rhodes
preached for me in Zion church & I baptised one child
The fourth Sunday he preached for me at Hollow creek.
on Wednesday the 27 of April I buried Saml Kerick &
preached from 1 Cor 15.19. The first Sunday in May

Mr. Rhodes preached in St. Johns & I baptised one child & in the afternoon in St. Jacobs church, I baptised Nancies child & buried a child in the sandhills. The 3 Sunday Mr Rhods preached in Zion ch & I baptised one child & in the afternoon we attended at St. Peters & I baptised 5 children. The fourth Sunday Mr Rhodes P in Salem church. The 5 Sunday Mr. Rhodes P in Bethlehem
The first Sunday in June Mr. Rhodes P at Mr. Jacob Mayers & I baptised one child. The second Sunday in June at St. Johns & St Jacob & baptised one child The 3 Sunday in Zion & in the afternoon in St. Peters & baptised one child. The 4 Sunday in Salem & I preached from 1 Peter 3.15 & baptised one adult & one child & in the afternoon in St. Pauls & bapt. one child. Thursday the 30 of June I buried Henry Sease & P from Heb 2.15 & baptised one child.
The first Sunday in July I P at J. Mayers from the Epistle Rom 6.3-11 & baptised one child. The second Sunday in July I P in St. Johns from the gospel Mark 8.1-9 & baptised 2 children & Mr. Rhodes in St. Jacobs. I P on the 3 Sunday in July in Zion Ch from the gospel Mat 7.15-23 & baptised 3 children.
The 4 Sunday in July I P in Salem from the 1 Cor 6-13 & baptised one child. Thursday the 28 of July I buried Wm Lybrands daughter

Page 136: & preached from Rev. 14.13. The 5 Sunday in July I P in Bethlehem ch from Heb 2.15 & baptised 2 children. The first Sunday in August I P at Jacob Mayers from the gospel Luke 18.9-14.
Monday the 8 buried Henry Earigles daughter & preached from Mark 10.14.
Friday 12 1842 buried John Miller & preached from Ps 39.4. The second Sunday in August P in St. Jacobs Ch from the epistle 2 Cor 3.4-11 & baptised one child. Saturday the 20 P in St. Peters from the gospel Luke 10.23-37. The 3 Sunday preached from the same in Zion The fourth Sunday in St. Pauls, little hollow creek, from the epistle Gal. 5.16-24 & baptised one child & in the afternoon I buried George Oswalts Wife & P from Rev. 14.13 & on Monday Buried Adam Shealys son Josiah & George Holtawanger Junr preached from John 11.25. Sept 1842 Eaffie's second child was born on the 5 Sunday in July 1842. The first Sunday in Sept I P at J Mayers from the epistle Gal. 6.1.
Wednesday the 7 of Sept P the funeral for Thos Fricks daughters from Rev. 21.4.
Friday the 9 P for John George Lindler from Heb. 4.3. The Second Sunday in Sept I P in St. Johns from the gospel Luke 7.11-17 & in the afternoon from the in (sic) St. Jacobs & baptised one child.
Monday the 12 I buried Magdalen Stoutmyers daughter & preached from Heb 4.3.
Saturday the 17 buried the Widow See & p from Heb 4.3. The 3 Sunday in Septr

Page 137: I P in Zion from the epistle Ephes 4.1-6 & in the afternoon in St. Peters where Stroble P for me & I baptised one child.
Saturday the 24 buried David Millers son & p from 2 Cor. 5.1

The 4 Sunday I attended at Salem hollowcreek & was
requested to bury Uriah Crouts child & P from Heb. 4.3.
Wednesday the 28 buried David Koons son & P from Eccles
12.7.
Saturday the first of October 1842 buried Warrens wife
& P from Eccles 12.7.
The first Sunday in Octr I P at J. Mayers from the gospel Mat 9.1-8 & baptised one child.
Thursday the 6 of Octr buried David Chapman & p from
John 5.24. The second Sunday I P in St. John from the
gospel Mat 22.1-14 & baptised one child & in the afternoon P from Luke 14.17 & baptised one child.
Monday the 10 buried George Slices child & P from Luke
8.52. The 3 Sunday I P in Zion from the gospel St.
John 4.47-54 & in the afternoon from the same in St.
Peters.
The 4 Sunday I P in Salem from Gal. 2-28 & baptised 5
children & in the afternoon from the same in St. Pauls
Wednesday the 26 Buried Daniel Younginer & P from Job
14.7.
Friday the 28 I buried John Myers Daughter Mary & P
from Ps 139.4.
The 5 Sunday in October I P in Bethlehem from Rom 13.
10
The first Sunday in Novr 1842 I P at J Mayers from the
epistle Col. 1.9-14 & baptised 5 children. Wednesday
the 9 I P. buried Mary Settsler & P from 2 Tim 1.10.

Page 138: Thursday the 10 of Novr 1842 I P a Thanksgiving Sermon
in Bethlehem from Phil 4.6. & baptised one child.
The second Sunday in St. John from the epistle 1 Thes
4.13-18 & from the same in St. Jacobs in the afternoon.
Monday the 14 buried John Mayers Daughter Anna Catherine
& P from Rom 8.18.
Thursday the 15 some of my friends & myself attended
the Synod at St. Marks Church Edgefield.
The third Sunday Jacob Kleckly preached for me in Zion
church & I baptised Killians child.
The fourth Sunday in Salem church a funeral sermon for
David Taylers child from Heb 4.3. & baptised 5 children.
Saturday the 3 of Decr 1842 buried Henry Hendrixs daughter & P from Rom 8.18.
The first Sunday in Decr at Jacob Mayers from the epistle Rom 15.4-13 & baptised 3 children.
The 3 Sunday in Decr in Zion from Mat 11.5 & baptised
one child & in the afternoon from the same in St.
Peters.
Thursday the 22 buried Jacob Earigles wife & P from
1 Cor 15.53 & baptised one child. The 4 Sunday being
Christmas day at Salem from the gospel Luke 2.1-14 &
baptised 3 children & in the afternoon in St. Pauls
from the same.
The first Sunday in January 1843 in St. Peters piney
woods from the gospel Luke 2.21
On Tuesday burried David Lindlers child & P from Rom
6.23.
Thursday the 12 buried Eve Earigle & preached from 2
Cor 5.1 & in the evening Married Maintam (?) See to
Caroline Wessinger & also at the same time married
George Drafts to Lusinda Hendrix.

Page 139: On Friday the 6 of January 1843 being Epiphany I P in

Bethlehem from the gospel Mat 2.1-12 & baptised one child.
The second Sunday in St. Johns from the epistle Rom 12. 1-6 in the afternoon in st. Jacobs from 2 Tim 1.10 it being a funeral Sermon for William Risters child & I baptised 3 children.
Wednesday 11 buried Michael Lindlers child & P from St. John 14.3
Friday the 13 buried Michaels Linders Wife & P from Col. 3.4. The 3 Sunday in January in Zion from Rom. 12.4.5. baptised 3 children & Married Daniel Cromer to Julian Monts & in the afternoon in St. Peters from Heb 4.2. The 4 Sunday in Salem from the gospel Mat 8.1-13 baptised 5 children & Married Wilm. Lindler to Elisabeth Earigle & in the afternoon in St Pauls from Mat 8.10
Thursday 26 Married Albert Hook to Ann Drafts & baptised one child. The 5 Sunday in Bethlehem from the gospel Mat 8.23-27 & in the evening Married Benj. Sligh to Sally Koon also Jesse Wessinger to Panilipy Coogler & baptised 4 children.
Tuesday the 31 of Jany burried David Fikes son & P from Mat 25.46.
Thursday the 2 of Feby Married Hirem Jackson to Sarah Amick.
The first Sunday in Feby preached in St. Peters from the gospel Mat 13.24-30 baptised one child. The second Sunday Married Adam Haltawanger to Harriet Ray & preached in St. John from the gospel Mat 20.1-16 & baptised 2 children.

Page 140: & in the afternoon in St. Jacobs from the gospel Mat. 20.1-16.
Monday the 13 of Feby 1843 buried Henry Earigles son & P from Rev. 14.13.
Thursday the 16 of Feby Married Lemuel Gaminer to Jane Caroline Franklow.
Sunday morning the 19 buried Noah Corley & preached from Heb. 4.3. after which, I preached in Zion from the Gospel Luke 8.4-15 & in the afternoon from the same in St. Peters.
Tuesday 21 burried James Balentines daughter & P from Rev. 14.13.
The 4 Sunday in Septr (sic) in Salem from the gospel Luke 18.31-43 & baptised 2 children & in the afternoon from the same in St. Pauls.
On Monday buried Dr. Koons child & preached from Rev. 14.13 & baptised one child.
The first Sunday in March The Rev. Mr. Hull preached for me in St. Peters church on Friday the 10 buried George Wingard & Mr Hull preached. The second Sunday prevented on account of rain. The 3 Sunday Mr Hull preached for me in Zion & I baptised 2 children.
Wednesday the 22 buried Jacob Amicks Son & preached from 1 Cor 15.19
Thursday the 23 Married John P. Earhart to Anna Lybrand. The 4 Sunday preached in Salem ch from the epistle Gal. 4.21-31 & baptised 4 children & in the afternoon from the same in St. Pauls and baptised one child.

Page 141: Wednesday 29 buried Mr. Stucks grand son & preached from 1 Cor 15.19

In St. Peters on the first Sunday in April 1843 from the gospel John 8.46-59 & baptised 4 children.
The second Sunday in St. John from the gospel Mat 21.109 & in the afternoon from the same in St. Jacobs.
Goodfriday in Bethlehem from Rom 4.25.
Saturday 15 Buried Mrs. Bickley & preached from 2 Cor 5.14.15
Easter Sunday in Zion from Col. 3.1. Confirmed 10 baptised one child & one adult & administered the Sacrament to 115 Communicants.
Thursday the 20 Married Emanuel Oswalt to Ruhem (?) Lewey. Friday 21 P the funeral for David Oswalts children & P from 2 Cor 5.14.15.
Saturday P at preparatory Sermon in Salem Church from Rom 7.20 & baptised 2 children. The 4 Sunday P from 1 John 5.10 Confirmed 8 & administered the Sacrament to 95.
The first Sunday in May 1843 from the gospel in St. Peters & baptised one child. The second Sunday in St. John from the gospel John 16.5-15 & baptised one child. & Married Jacob Earigle to Elisabeth Shealy & in the afternoon from the same in St. Jacobs.
The 3 Sunday in Zion from the gospel John 16.23-30 & baptised 5 children & in the afternoon from the same in St. Peters.
Tuesday evening 23 Married Thomas Bouknight to

Page 142: Mary Magdalen Sligh.
Ascension day P in Bethlehem from Mark 16.14-20 & baptised 2 children. The Sunday after Ascension in St. Pauls on Saturday from Mat 5.4. & baptised 2 children.
Sunday from 1 Cor 10.15.16 & administered the Sacrament to 1 & in the afternoon in Salem from John 16.27 & baptised 2 children.
The first Sunday in June, being Whitsunday in St. Peters from the gospel John 14.23-31 & baptised 3 children.
The 2 Sunday in June in St. Johns from the gospel St. John 3.1-15 & baptised 1 child & in the afternoon from the same in St. Jacobs & baptised one child.
The 3 Sunday in Zion from the gospel Luke 16.19-31 & baptised 2 children & in the afternoon from the same in St. Peters & baptised 2 children. The 4 Sunday in Salem from the gospel Luke 14.16-24 & baptised 3 children. The 1 Sunday in July 1843 in St. Peters from the gospel Luke 15.1-10 baptised 3 children.
Thursday 6 Buried George Oswalts daughter & preached from Rom 6.23. The second Sunday in St. Johns preached the funeral for Miss Miller from Rev. 14.13 & in the afternoon in St. Jacob from the epistle Rom 8.18 & baptised one child & on Monday the 10 buried Widow Epting & P from 1 Cor 15.55. The 3 Sunday in Zion preached a funeral for James Carr from Rev. 14.13 & in the afternoon

Page 143: buried 2 of George Oswalts children & preached from 1 Cor 15.55. The 4 Sunday in July in Salem from the epistle Rom 6.3-11 & in the afternoon from the same in St. Paul. The 5 Sunday in Bethlehem on Saturday from 1 Cor 11.28 & on Sunday from 1 Cor 10.15.16 & administered the Sacrament.
Monday 31 Buried Rubin(?) Wingards son & preached from Job 1.21

Thursday the 3 of August Married James Stone to Catherine Stack. Friday the 4 in Zion a Thanksgiving sermon from Ps 136.1. The first Sunday in August in piney wood church from the gospel Mat 7.15-23. The Second Sunday in St. Johns from the gospel Luke 16.1-9 & baptised 5 children & in the afternoon from the same in St. Jacobs
Friday the 11 Burried old Lewis George & P from 2 Cor 5.1
The 3 Sunday in August in Zion from St. John 3.7 & in the afternoon from the same in St. Peters
Monday the 21 Buried Harris & P from 1 Cor 15.55 & baptised 1 child. The 4 Sunday in Salem Married Absalom Jackson to Nancy Earigle & preached from St. John 3.7 & baptised one child.
Tuesday the 29 burried Mrs. Tayler & preached from Heb 2.15. Thursday the 31 burried Mrs. Wheeler & preached from Heb. 2.15 & baptised 2 children.

Page 144: & in the afternoon George Oswalt was married to the Widow Bryson.
The first Sunday in Sept 1843 in St. Peters from the epistle 2 Cor 3.4-9. The 2 Sunday in St. John from the gospel Luke 10.23-37 & baptised one child & in the afternoon from the same in St. Jacobs.
The 3 Sunday prevented on account of high water. Wednesday Buried Adam Schwartzes child & preached from 1 Tim 6.7. & on Thursday 21 gave Uriah Mayer the Sacrament. The 4 Sunday in Septr in Salem from the gospel Mat 6.24-34 & baptised 1 child & in the afternoon from the same in St. Paul.
Monday 24 Buried Michael Summer & preached from Heb 4.3.
First (sic) Sunday in Septr 1843 in S
the gospel Luke 7.11-17 & baptised two children. The 2 Sunday in St. John from the gospel Luke 14.1-11 & in the afternoon from the same in St. Jacobs & baptised one child. Thursday the 12 of Septr Married David Griffith & Elisabeth Hook. The 3 Sunday in Zion Church from the gospel Mat 22.34-46 & baptised one child & in the afternoon from the same in St. Peters.
Thursday the 19 Buried John Stoutemyers son & P from St. John 11.25. The 4 Sunday in <u>October</u> in Salem ch from the gospel Mat 9.1-8 & <u>baptised one</u> child & in the afternoon from the same in St. Pauls.
Tuesday the 24 Buried Stephen Bowers wife & preached from 1 Cor 15.55. The 5 Sunday in Bethlehem from the gospel Mat 22.1-14.

Page 145: baptised one child. Thursday the 14 of November 1839 Married Daniel Corley to Jany Boney.

The middle row is Rutherfords Pew. The next above is the Dwarf Marrowfat (?) (Russel) & the 3 row is the blue Imperial & the 4 row is drawf marrow fat & the blue Imperial, all of (Russell).

Sermons	1891
Baptisms	1591
Confirmations	651
Matrimonies	219
Ordinations	2

John has continued the Rale Road since the first of
January. June & Joe commenst working on Monday the
15 of Feby 1841. S. S. took them down on the first
Sunday in March. S. S. went to the R. R. on his own
record. May the 24 1841 I recd 100 Dollars toward
their work. Joe left the Rail road on the first of
July. Sinah & loid went off on the first of August.

Page 146: Recd May 15 1838 from the Rev. Adam Miller 25 Doz
of the Constituions at 18 Cents each.
I paid Mr. Miller in advance $5 & he owes me for books
that was sold $1 37½

Constitution & 2 Minutes one to Henry Kinard & one of
the constitutions.

(upside down on page--comment on Rom 10.4.)

Page 147: ___ Sunday in Novr 1843 in St. Peters from the gospel
St. John 4.47-5 & baptised 1 child & in the afternoon
Buried Mrs. David Chapmans Daughter & preached from 2
Cor 4.17.18 & on Wednesday 8 buried David Craps son &
preached from the same & on Thursday the 9 buried Frank
Koons Wife & preached from Job 5.26. The 2 Sunday in
St. John from the gospel Mat 18.23-35 & in the after-
noon from the same in St. Jacobs. The 3 Sunday in Zion
from the gospel Mat 22.15-22 & in the afternoon in St.
Peters from Acts 16.30.
Tuesday the 21 Buried Uriah Mayer & preached from Job.
5. 26.
Wednesday the 22 buried Reubin Wingards son & P from
2 Cor 4.17.18. The 4 Sunday in Salem from the gospel
Mat 9.18-26 & baptised 2 children & in the afternoon in
St. Paul from Acts 16.30.
Thursday the 30 of Novr Married Reubin Corley to Mar-
garet Catharine Sox. The first Sunday in Decr in St.
Peters from 1 Thes 4.13.
Wednesday 6 Baptised Daniel Metzes son.
The second Sunday in Decr preached a funeral sermon
for George Eptings children in Laurence Dist. from
1 Cor 15.55 & baptised 2 children.
Thursday the 14 buried Henry Millers son & preached
from Rom 6.23.
The 3 Sunday in Zion from the gospel Mat 11.2-11 &
baptised 2 children & on Monday the 18 buried Dr. Koons
daughter & in the afternoon buried George Ballentines
(from Ephes 4.5 & baptised 1 child.)

Page 148: son & preached from Rom 6.23 for ____.
4.13.
Thursday 21 1843 Married George Mo (nts?) to Mary Luesia
Mathias.
The 4 Sunday in Salem from the gospel John 1.19-28
baptised 3 children & Married Henry Oxoner to one of
Risingers Daughters & in the afternoon from the same in
St. Pauls.
Christmas in St. Jacob from the gospel Luke 2.1-14 &
baptised 5 children. The 5 Sunday in Decr in Bethlehem
& preached the funeral for Mrs. Merryman from 2 Cor 5.1.
Buried Capt Wheelers child & P from Ec. 12.7.
The 6 of January 1844 being Epiphany preached from the
Gospel Mat 2.1-12 & baptised one child & on the first

Sunday in St. Peters from the epistle Rom 12.1-6 & baptised one child. The second Sunday in January in St. John from the gospel St. John 21.1-__ & in the afternoon from the same in St. Jacobs & baptised one child. The 3 Sunday in Zion from the gospel Mat 8.1-13 & in the afternoon from the same in St. Peters & baptised one child.
The 1 Sunday in Feby in St. Peters from the gospel Mat 20.1-16 & in the afternoon buried John Settsler & preached from Heb 13.14.
The 2 Sunday in St. John from the gospel & buried John Wicker & preached from 2 Cor 5.8 & in the afternoon in St. Jacobs from the gospel

Page 149:   __ 4-15.
Thursday the 15 of Feby 1844 Married Thomas Mathias to Joanna Bouknight & in the evening I married David Coogler to Sally Metz.
The 3 Sunday Married Jesse Sox to Martha Gable & preached from the gospel Luke 18.31-43 & baptised 3 children & in the afternoon from the same in St. Peters.
Saturday 24 buried Henry Nehemyer & preached from 2 Cor 5.8 & on the 4 Sunday in Salem from 2 Cor 5.8.9. a funeral sermon for Reubin Vansants child & baptised 2 children. & in the afternoon from 1 Cor 10.13 in St. Paul lower hollowcreek.
Thursday the 29 of Febry buried Thomas Bouknights wife & preached from 2 Cor 5.8.9. & on Saturday 2 of March preached the funeral for Sally Bowers child from 1 Cor 7.29-31.
The first Sunday in March in St. Peters from the gospel Mat 15.21-28. The 2 Sunday in March in St. John the gospel Luke 11.14-28 & baptised 4 children & in the afternoon in St. Jacob from Luke 11.24 & baptised one child. The 3 Sunday in Zion from the gospel St. John 6.1-15.
Monday the 18 buried Jacob Mayers son & P from 1 Tim 6.7. The 4 Sunday P at Samuel Holman's from Ephes 4.5 & baptised 1 child.

Page 150: Thursday the 28 of March 1844 Married ____ to Martha ann Elisabeth Sharp & on Saturday the 30 Buried Henry Minnick & preached from Rom 14.7.8.
Sunday the 31 P in Bethlehem from the epistle Phil 2.5-11.
Monday 1 of April Buried Slone & P from Rom 14.8.
Goodfriday P in Salem from Isa 53.6 & baptised 5 children & in the afternoon from the same in St. Pauls.
Easter Sunday in St. Peters from the gospel Mark 16.1-8 & baptised 5 children.
The 2 Sunday in St. John from the gospel St. John 20.19-31 & in St. Jacobs from the same in the afternoon.
The 3 Sunday in April in St. Peters or Metzes church from 1 Cor 11.28 & administered the Sacrament to 35 Comts. & recd 2 Members. The 4 Sunday Married Henry Kesler to Harriet Price & preached in Salem from the gospel St. John 16.16-23 & baptised 3 children & in the afternoon in St. Pauls from John 16.27. The first Saturday in May P in St. Peters from 1 Cor 11.28 Baptised 8 children & confirmed 66 Persons & on Sunday P from 1 John 3.1 & administered the Sacrament to 157 Communicants. The 2 Sunday in St. Johns from the gospel St. John 16.23-__ Confirmed 12 & administered the sa-

Page 151:
crament to 36.
Ascensions day in St. Jacobs Ch from the gospel Mark 16.14-20. Confirmed 7 & administered the sacrament to 38. The 3 Sunday in May P in Zion from 1 John 3.1. Confirmed 20 baptised 2 Adults one child & administered the Sacrament to 124.
Saturday 18 of May Buried Catharine Coogler P from 1 Tim 6.7.8.
The 4 Sunday in Salem on Saturday from 1 Cor 11.28. Baptised one adult & 3 children on Sunday Confirmed 7 & administerd the Sacrament to 85 & preached from the gospel John 14.23-31 & in the afternoon in St. Paul from 14.27.
On Whit Monday burried George Bundricks wife & P from Heb. 11.13.
Trinity Sunday being the 1 Sunday in June 1844 in St. Peters from the gospel St. John 3.1-15 & baptised 3 children. The 2 Sunday in St. Johns from the gospel Luke 16.19-31 & baptised 1 child & in the afternoon from the same in St. Jacobs.
On the Saturday before the 2 Sunday P a Sermon at Mrs. Amicks & gave her the Sacrament preached from St. Luke 19.10. The 3 Sunday in June in Zion from the epistle 1 John 3.13-18 & in the afternoon buried James Stones Wife & preached from Ps 9.2-5 & baptised one child.
Thursday 20 Buried Christian Sites & P from Heb. 18. 13. Saturday 22 P the funeral for one of Philip Aleywines children & preached from 2 Cor 5.15. The 4 Sunday at Salem Ch the funeral for old Mrs. Halman & P from Heb. 11.13 & in the afternoon in St. Pauls from Luke 15.7 & baptised 2 children.

Page 152:
The first Sunday in July 1844 in St ___ from the Epistle 1 Peter 3.8-15 & baptised one child The 2 Saturday at Martin Fikes from Ps 25.16-18. The 2 Sunday in St. John from Rom 8.16 & baptised one child & in the afternoon in St. Jacobs from Mat 5.20.
The 3 Sunday in Zion from the epistle Rom 6.19.25 & baptised 3 children & in the afternoon from the same in St. Peters & baptised one child. The 4 Sundayin Salem from the epistle Rom 8.12-17 & baptised 3 children & in the afternoon in St. Pauls from 1 Cor 2.14.
Thursday the 1 of August married Hirem Keasler to Emeline Elisabeth Frayser.
The first Sunday in August in St. Peters from the epistle 1 Cor 1.06-13 & baptised 2 children. The 3 Sunday in St. John from the epistle 1 Cor 13.1-11 & in the afternoon in St. Jacobs from the same & baptised one child. & elected elders. The 3 Sunday in Zion from the gospel Luke 18.9-14 & in the afternoon from the same in St. Peters & baptised one child.
Thursday the 22 buried Mrs. Chapmans daughter & preached from St. Mark 10.14 The 4 Sunday in Salem from the epistle 2 Cor 3.4-11 & baptised 1 child & in the afternoon from the same in St. Pauls.
Sunday morning married Isaiah Price to Barbara Caroline Keisler.
The first Sunday in Septr in St. Peters from the gospel Luke 10.23-37. The 2 Sunday in St. Johns from the gospel Luke 17.11-19 & in the after from the same in St. Jacobs. The 3 Sunday in Zion from the gospel Mat 6.24-34 & baptised 2 child.

Wednesday 11 buried Major Swigards child & preached from 2 Tim 1.10 & baptised 12 children.
Thursday 19 Married Thos Bouknight to Martha Ann Elisabeth Derick. The 4 Sunday in Salem from Mat 6. 24-34 &

Page 153: _____ in the afternoon in Little hollow Creek Church from Mat 6.33. The 5 Sunday in Bethlehem Rom 8. 3.4. The 1 Sunday in Octr in Peters from the epistle _ Cor 1.4-9 & baptised 2 children. The second Sunday In St. Johns from Mat 9.1-8 & in the after noon in St. Jacobs from the same & baptised 2 children. The 3 Sunday in Octr 1844 in Zion from Heb. 2.1 & baptised 1 child & in the afternoon from the same in St. Peters & baptised 1 child. The 4 Sunday in Octr in Salem from the gospel St. John 4.47-54 & baptised 3 children & in the afternoon from the same in St. Pauls & baptised 1 child. Thursday October 31 Married John Frederick Fulmer to Elisabeth Wheeler.
The 1 Sunday in Novr in St. Peters from Heb 2.1. & on Monday buried Win Eve's wife & preached from Ps 39.4. The 2 Sunday in St. Johns from the epistle Phil 3.7-21 & baptised one child & in the afternoon from the same in St. Jacobs & baptised 1 child. The 3 Sunday in Zion married William Whites to Mary Ann Leaphart & preached from Heb 13.4 & baptsed 2 children in the afternoon in St. Peters from Col. 1.9-14 & baptised 1 child.
Thursday 31 of Novr married Levi Boland to Mary Ann Wheeler. The 4 Sunday in Salem from Ephes 2.4-10 married Lewis Crout to Rebecca Risinger & baptised 3 children. in the afternoon preached the funeral for Michael Drafts from Ps 39.4 & baptised 1 child.
Tuesday 26 Married Joseph Price to Elisabeth Long.
Thursday 28 Married Henry Bryson to Elisa Swigard.
The 1 Sunday in Decr Rev. Mr. Peterson preached for me in St. Peters & also on the 2 Sunday in St. Johns & St. Jacobs on the 3 Sunday in Zion & I baptised 3 children Thursday 19 Married Thomas A. Wingard to Nancy Monts & baptised 1 child. & in the evening Married Ephriam Walter Boland to Susanna Bowers. Sunday morning 22 Married Napolian Gaminer

Page 154: to Sarah Gable & baptised 2 children. ON 5 Sunday ___ Bethlehem Church from Titus 2.11-14 & baptised 1 child. Thursday 26 of Decr 1844 Married Christian Rall to Nancy Julia Earhart. Thursday the 2 of January 1845 Buried Jacob Lindlers son & preached from Mat 11.
The first Sunday in January 1845 I preached in St. P--- from 1 Cor 9.11 & baptised 2 children on Monday being Epiphany in Bethlehem from 1 Cor 9.11.
Wednesday the 7 Buried John Lewey & preached from Luke 7.14. Thursday the 9 Married Joseph Sulton to Juliann Fulmer & on Friday the 10 buried Enoch Grubbs & preached from St. John 5.25. Saturday 11 Buried Elias Taylers son & preached from St. John 5.25 & baptised 1 child. The 2 Sunday in St. Johns from 1 Cor 9.11 & in the afternoon from the same in St. Jacobs & on Monday morning baptised 1 slave.
Tuesday the 14 Buried old Mrs. Wingard & preached from St. John 8.51. The 4 Sunday in January in Salem from 3 Peter 2.7 & baptised 1 child & in the afternoon from 1 Tim 2.4.

Saturday the 1 of Feby 1845 buried Levi Shealys child & preached from Ps 39.4 & in the afternoon buried his mother in law Mrs. Earigle & preached from St. John 5.25 & on the first Sunday in St. Peters from 2 Peter 3.9 & baptised one child. Tuesday 4 Married Artimas Earigle to Ann Elisabeth (?) Price. Thursday the 6 Married James Allen Bickly (?) to Mary Ann Wessinger. Sarahs child was born on Tuesday night the 4 of Febry 1845. on the __ Sunday in St. Johns from 2 Peter 3.9 & in the afternoon from the same in St. Jacobs on Tuesday the 11 of Febry Married George Metz to Elisabeth Sease. Saturday 15 Buried old John Corley (?)

Page 155: _____ 8.42. Isa 57.2 & Heb 11.10 on the 3 Sunday in Feby 1845 in Zion from 2 Peter _.9 & baptised 2 children & in the afternoon from the same in St. Peters & baptised 1 child. The 4 Sunday in Salem from Ephes 5.8 & in the afternoon from the same in St. Paul Friday 28 of Febry buried Jacob Crim & preached from Eccl. 12.7 & baptised 1 child.
The first ___ in March in St. Peters from Ephes 5.8. The 2 Sunday in St. John from the gospel John 8.46-59 & in the afternoon from the same in St. Jacobs & baptised 1 child. The 3 Sunday in Zion from the epistle Phil 2.5-11 & baptised 2 children & in the afternoon in St. Peters from Col 1.19. Thursday 20 of March 1845 Married Daniel Shealy to Rosena Frick & baptised one child.
Goodfriday in Zion from Col 1.19 & baptised one child & in the afternoon gave the Sacrament to old Mr Ramick
on Saturday afternoon preached at old Mr. Shealys on Hollow Creek from Mat 11.28. Sunday morning being Easter gave old Mrs Riseinger the Sacrament & preached in Salem church from Col3.1 & baptised 5 children. Easter Monday in St. Peters.
Saturday 29 Buried Daniel Kleckleys Daughter & Preached from Ps 103.13. The 5 Sunday in March in Bethlehem from the gospel John 20.19-31. The 1 Sunday in April in St. Peters from the gospel John 10.11-16 & baptised 1 child. 2 Sunday in April in St. Johns from 1 Peter 2.24 baptised 3 children & in the afternoon in St. Jacobs from the same & baptised 1 child.
Saturday 19 of April in St. Pauls church from 1 John 1.9 & baptised 2 children. on Sunday the 20 from 1 Cor 11.28 & administered the Sacrament in St. Pauls church little hollow creek

Page 156: & in the afternoon in St. Peters from _____ & baptised 2 children.
Tuesday 22 Buried John Risinger & preached from St. John 5.25
Thursday 24 Buried John Bouknight Junr & preached from 2 Tim 1.1.10 & in the afternoon Married John Leonard Sease to Martha Elisabeth Fikes. The 4 Sunday in April in Salem from Heb 2.15 & baptised 3 children & the Saturday before at old Adam Shelys from Mar 1.15 & on Sunday afternoon in St. Pauls from Mark 1.15.
The 1 Sunday in May in St. Peters from Gal. 5.1 & baptised 4 children & one black child & in the afternoon at Martin Fiks from 34 Ps & 19 verse.
The second Sunday in St. Johns & Buried John Setzler &

& preached from St. John 5.25 & baptised one child &
on Monday buried Jacob Bundrick & preached from 1 Cor
15.19. The Saturday before the 3 Sunday preached a
preparatory Sermon in Zion from 1 John 1.9.
Sunday from 1 Cor 11.28 & administered the Sacrament
to 103 & baptised 2 children.
The 24 of May in Salem from 1 John 1.9 & baptised 3
adults & in the afternoon at Adam Shealies from Gal.
5.1 & on Sunday in Salem from Mat 26.26-29. Confirmed
43 & administered the Sacrament to 170.
Friday 30 buried Radama Riseinger & preached from Mat
24.44. Sunday the first of June 1845 in Peters church
from the gospel Luke 16.19-31 baptised 1 child in the
afternoon preached the funeral for David Kunkles child
from Mat 24.44 & on Monday the 24 buried Nathan Williamsons wife & preached from the 39 Ps & 4 verse.

Page 157: _____ buried Uriah Crouts child & preached from Col. 3.4.
The 2 Sunday preached the funeral Alexander Commalanders
child from Heb 4.3 & baptised one child also in St. Johns
preached the funeral for Mrs. Bundricks daughter from
Ps 39.4 & in the afternoon in St. Jacobs from the gospel
Luke 15.1-10 & baptised one child. The 3 Sunday in
June in Zion from the gospel Luke 6.36-42. Baptised 2
children & in the afternoon in St. Peters from Col 1.23
& baptised 3 children. Saturday the 22 of June at
Adam Shelys from St. John 4.24 & on Sunday in Salem from
St. John 8.31.32 & in the afternoon in St. Pauls from
John 8.31 & Inaugurated John Price & Oswalt as Elders &
on Tuesday 26 Buried Andrew Geigers son & preached from
St. John 5.25 & baptised one child & on the 5 Sunday in
Bethlehem from Gal. 2.20 & baptised one adult.
Thursday the 3 of July 1845 buried Adam Amicks daughter
& preached from St. John 5.25.
First Sunday in July in St. Peters from the gospel Mark
8.1-9. The 2 Sunday in St. John from the epistle Rom
8.12-17 & inaugurated George Chapman, the afternoon from
the same in St. Jacobs & baptised 2 children.
Tuesday 15 Buried John Roofs wife & preached from 2 Tim
1.10. The 3 Sunday in Zion from the epistle 1 Cor 10.
6-13 & baptised one child & in the afternoon from the
same when Mr. Danner attended in St. Peters.
Wednesday 23 buried William See & preached from Ps
39.4 & on Thursday 24 Buried Adam Earhart & preached
from Rom 6.23. Saturday 26 preached at

Page 158: Adam Shealys from _____ where Mr. Paton preached
for me, I baptised 14 children & in the afternoon in
St. Paul from Gal. 3.10. The first Saturday in August
1845 in St. Peters from Luke 18.9-14 & baptised one
child
on the first Sunday at a Schoolhouse near Stephen Bowers
in Newberry from 2 Tim 4.2. The Second Sunday in St.
John where Mr. Donner preached & I baptised 2 childr
& in the afternoon in St. Jacob. Mr Danner preached.
Tuesday 12 Buried David Clapps Daughter & preached from
2 Tim 1.10. The 3 Sunday in Zion from the gospel Luke
10.23-37 & baptised one child & Mr. Danner preached German & in the afternoon in St. Peters & on Saturday
before the 4 Sunday at Mr. Adam Shealys & on the 4 Sunday in Salem from the epistle Gal. 5.16-24 & baptised
2 children. The 5 Sunday in Bethlehem from Col 1.12-14

& baptised one child.
The 1 Sunday in Septr 1845 from the epistle Ephes 3.13-21 & baptised one child. The 2 Sunday in St. John from the gospel Luke 14.1-11 & baptised 1 child & in the afternoon from the same in St. Jacobs & baptised 2 children. The 3 Sunday in Zion Mr. Danner preached I exhorted & married Abel Platt to Caroline Shull. The 4 Sunday in Salem from Gal. 2.17 Baptised 2 children & in the afternoon in St. Pauls from Mat 9.2 & baptised 2 children & married Emanuel Shealy to Rebeca Price.
The first Sunday in Ocr. 1845 in St. Peters from the gospel Mat 22.1-14 & baptised one child. The 2 Sunday in St. John from the gospel St. John 4.47-54 & in the afternoon in St. Jacobs from the same. The 3 Sunday in Zion from Heb 13.9 Baptised one child & Married John Bell to Mary Sox. Wednesday the 15 Buried Wilm. Shulls daughter & preached from Mat 18.3

Page 159: Sunday in the afternoon in St. Peters from Heb 13. 9 & baptised 2 children
The 4 Sunday preached Saml Wingards Funeral from 2 Tim 4.7.8.
The 1 Sunday in Novr 1845 in Bethlehem from the gospel Mat 8.18-26. The 2 Sunday in St. Johns from Isa 26.3 & baptised 1 child & in the afternoon from the same in St. Jacobs & baptised 1 child.
The 3 Sunday in Zion preached from the gospel Mat 25.31-46 & baptised 1 child
Saturday 22 preached at old Adam Shealys from Isa 26.3
The 4 Sunday in Salem from the epistle 1 Thes 5.1-11 & baptised 4 children. Saturday the 29 buried one of Michael Corleys children & preached from Rev. 14.13 & baptised one child. Sunday in Bethlehem church from the epistle Rom 13.11-14 & baptised one cullerd[sic] child & preached from Mark 10.14. Thursday 11 married John Koon to Margaret Elisabeth Bauknight, & baptised one child. Friday 12 buried Noah Halman & preached from Phil 1.21. The 2 Sunday in St. Pauls from the gospel Mat 11.2-11. The 3 Sunday Married Laban H. Trapp to Mary Bouknight & then preached in Zion from the epistle Phil 4.4-7.
Tuesday the 23 Married Henry Kleckly to Sally Monts. Christmas preached in St. Peters piney wood from the gospel Luke 2.1-14 & baptised 1 child. The 4 Sunday in St. Jacobs from the epistle Gal 4.1-7 & baptised 2 children.

Page 160: New Years day 1846 Mr. Moser preached in Zion.
First Sunday in January 1846 in Bethlehem from Titus 3.4-7. Friday the 9 Buried George Wessingers son & preached from 1 Tim 6-8.
The 2 Sunday in St. Johns & baptised 1 child.
Thursday 15 Married David Bookman to Mary Rall.
The 3 Sunday in Peters or Meetzes church from Rom 12.16. Saturday 24 at Adam Shealys from 1 Cor 3.11 on Sunday in Salem from 1 Cor 1.10 & baptised 3 children. Sunday evening 25 married Richard Bickley to Mary Lindler.
The first Sunday in April 1846 in St. Peters from 1 Cor 3.11 & baptised one child. The 2 Sunday Married William Shealy to Susanna Lominick & then preached in St. Pauls church from the gospel Mat 20.1-16 &

baptised one child & in the afternoon preached the funeral for Reuben Crout from Rom 6.23. The 3 Sunday in Zion from the gospel Luke 7.4-15 & baptised 4 children. Tuesday 17 buried Clarisa Slone. Thursday 19 Married Jesse Roof to Margaret Shull & baptised one child. The 4 Sunday in St. Jacob from the gospel Luke 18 31-43 & baptised 3 children. Sunday morning the first of March Married John Middleton Boland to Anna Barbara Frick & Mr Moser preached in St. Peters piney wood. Thursday the 5 of March Married Uriah George Wessinger to Mary Ann Sikes. The 2 Sunday Mr Moser preached in St. Johns & I baptised 2 children. Monday 9 of March Buried Benjamin Roof & preached from Mat 24.44. The 3 Sunday in St. Peters or Meetzes church from the epistle Ephes 5.8. The Saturday before the 4 Sunday at Adam Shealys Mr. Moser preached & I baptised 2 children & on the 4 Sunday Mr Moser & Mr Davis preached & I baptised 4 children.

Page 161: The 5 Sunday in March 1846 I married Joseph Bookman to Milly Weed & baptised 2 children I then preached in Bethlehem church from Gal 4.21 & baptised one child & in the afternoon at John Elisers from 2 Cor 4.17 & on Tuesday 31 of March I burried John Eleser & preached from Heb 2.6.
The 1 Sunday in April in St. Peters & baptised 4 children. On Goodfriday in St. Pauls & baptised one child. Easter Sunday in Zion Mr. Moser preached & I baptised 6 children, Confirmed 5 & administered the Sacrament to 102 Communicants. on Monday in St. Jacobs & baptised 1 child on Monday the 6 of April buried young Sulton & preached from 2 Cor 5.1. The 3 Sunday in St. Peters or Metzes church & administered the Sacrament & Confirmed 3 Persons the 4 Sunday in St. Jacobs from the epistle 1 Peter 2.21-25 & baptised one child.
The 1 Sunday in May in Bethlehem from Col 1.21-23 & baptised 1 child & 5 black children.
Wednesday the 6 of May Buried John Baitys child & preached from Rev. 14.13 & on Thursday the 7 of May Married Hirem Addy to Elisa Craps. The 3 Sunday in St. Peters or Meetzes Church from John 16.27
The 4 Sunday in St. Jacobs & administered the Sacrament & Confirmed 13
Whitsunday in St. John administered the Sacrament & Confirmed 3.
Whitmonday in St. Peters or piney wood & baptised 2 children. The first Sunday in June in Salem & baptised 1 child. Saturday 13 buried Jacob Long & preached from 2 Tim 1.10. The 2 Sunday in St. Pauls

Page 162: from the gospel Luke 16.19-31 & baptised 1 child. The 3 Sunday in Zion from Zion from the gospel Luke 14.16-24. The 4 Sunday in St. Jacobs from the gospel Luke 15.1-10. The 1 Sunday in July in Bethlehem from Luke 6.36.4_. The 2 Sunday in St. John from the epistle 1 Peter 3.8-22 & baptised 1 child.
The 3 Sunday in St. Peters from the epistle Rom 6.19-23 baptised 5 children & in the afternoon burried Daniel Drafts wife & preached from Rev. 14.13. Thursday 30 burried John Vansants wife & preached from John 6.47.
Saturday 1 of August preached a thanksgiving Sermon

in Salem from Ps 136.1
The 1 Sunday in August 1846 in Piney wood church from
the epistle Rom 8.12-17 & baptised 4 children. Wednesday 5 Buried John Whites wife & preached from John
6.47. The 2 Sunday in St. Pauls from Luke 16.1-9.
The 3 Sunday in Zion from the epistle 1 Cor 12.1-11
& baptised 1 child.
The 4 Sunday in St. Jacob from the gospel Luke 18.9-14
& baptised 2 children.
The first Sunday in Septr in Bethlehem from the epistle Gal. 3.15-22.
Tuesday the 8 buried David Amicks Daughter and preached
from Luke 8.52 & in the afternoon Buried George Addys
wife & preached from Gen 3.19.
The 2 Sunday in St. Johns from the epistle Gal. 5.16-
24 & baptised 3 children & in the afternoon Buried
George Slices son & preached from Mark 10.15.
Tuesday 15 Buried old Mrs. Gartman & preached from 2
Timothy 1.10. The 3 Sunday in Meetzes church from
the gospel Mat 6.24-34.
Saturday 26 Preached at Adam Shealy's from Mat 6.10
Baptised 2 children.

Page 163:   ___ Septr 1846 in Salem church from Rom 5.1 & baptised
2 children. Monday 28 buried John Hipp & preached
from Rom 6.23 & baptised 2 children. The first Sunday
in October Buried Uriah Wessinger & preached from Heb
4.3 & then Preached in the Pineywood Church from Ephes
4.1-6 & baptised 1 child. In the afternoon preached
the funeral for John Jacob Long from Heb. 4.3.
Thursday 8 preached at Mrs. Amicks from 25 Ps verse
16-18 & gave her the sacrament.
Saturday 10 Buried William Mabus son & preached from
Rom 6.23 & baptised 1 child. The 2 Sunday in St. Johns
from 1 Tim 2.4 & in the afternoon from the same in St.
Jacobs. The 3 Sunday in Zion from the gospel Mat 9.1-
8 & baptised 2 children & in the afternoon from the
same in St. Peters & baptised 1 child. Thursday 22
Buried Miss Mary Rinehart & preached from Mark 9.24.
Saturday 24 Preached in Salem from Mark 1.15 baptised
1 child & 1 adult & in the afternoon at Adam Shealys
from Mat 9.2. The 4 Sunday in Salem from Mat 22.1-14
Confirmed 9 administered the Sacrament to 117 & baptised 1 child.
Monday 26 buried Gabriel Wingard & preached from Rom
6.23 & in the afternoon at his Fathers from 1 Cor 15.55
The 1 Sunday in Novr 1846 in Bethlehem from the gospel
John 4.47-54 & baptised 1 child.
Tuesday 3 of Novr buried Rebecca Lybrand daughter of
Martin Lybrand & preached from Ps 39.4.
Friday 6 buried Aberhart Fulmer & preached from Ps
71.7.8. The 2 Sunday in St. Pauls from the gospel
Mat 18.23-35 & baptised 1 child. Monday 9 buried
Adam Shulls son & preached from

Page 164:   34.19. The 3 Sunday in Novr 1846 in St. P--- from
___ 2.3. The 4 Sunday in St. Jacobs from the gospel
Mat 9.18-26. The 5 Sunday(buried George Eliasers son)
P in St. Johns from 1 Thes 4.13-18 & baptised one
child.
The 1 Sunday in Decr in St. Peters from 1 Tim 1.15
& baptised 4 children. on the 2 Sunday in St. Johns

from Mat 1.21 & in the afternoon buried George Epting
& preached from John 11.25. Thursday 17 Married
Henry Wessinger to Luesia Lybrand & Friday 18 buried
Anna Margaret Gartman & preached from John 11.25. The
3 Sunday the Rev. E. Rudisal preached in Zion I baptised 3 children
Christmas day he preached in St. Peters & I baptised 1
child. Thursday 24 Married Jacob Lindler to Sally
Earigle & baptised 1 child. The 4 Sunday in Salem
he preaached & I baptised 2 children. The Saturday
before I baptised 2 children On Tuesday 29 he preached
in Zion & I baptised 1 child The first Sunday in
January 1847 Dr. Rudisill preached in St. Peters.
Thursday the 7 of January Married Daniel Shealy to
Sally Balentine. The 2 Sunday in St. Pauls from Rom
12.1-6. The 3 Sunday in St. Peters from St. John 2.
1-11. The 4 Sunday in St. Jacobs Mat 8.1-13 & baptised
one child. Thursday 28 of January Married Daniel
Kook to Epsy Senn & in the evening married Joel Tayler
to Mariah Lephart. The 5 Sunday in Zion from Col. 1.14
Thursday the 4 of Febry Married Aaron Brassell to Sally
Senn. Saturday 6 Buried George Crapps & preached from
1 Cor 15.55.
The 1 Sunday in Febry in St. Peters from the gospel Luke
8.4-15.

Page 165: _____ of February 1847 Married Joshua McCarty to
Anna Lindler. The 2 Sunday in St. John from the gospel
Luke 18.31-43.
Thursday the 18 Married Elias Frick to Lusinda Lybrand.
The 3 Sunday in Zion from the gospel Mat 4.1-11 &
baptised one child. The 4 Saturday at Adam Shealys from
Rom 4.8 & on Sunday in Salem from the gospel Mat 15.21-
28 & baptised 2 children.
Thursday 4 of March Married Wilm. Price to Elinder
Keisler.
The 1 Sunday in March at Bethlehem from Rom 8.1
Thursday the 18 Buried one of Andrew George's children
& preached from Mark 10.14. Monday 22 Buried John
Bells child & preached from Rom 5.12. The 4 Sunday
in St. Jacobs from Rom 8.1 & baptised one child.
On Goodfriday in Zion from Isa 53.5 & baptised 1 child
Easter Sunday in Piney wood from the gospel Mark 16.
1-8 & baptised 1 child.
On Saturday the 3 of April Buried Daniel Oxoners
daughter & preached from Rom 5.12.
Saturday 10 Buried old Mrs. Fike & preached from 2
Tim 4.7.8.
The 2 Sunday in St. Johns from the gospel St. John
20.19-31 & baptised 1 child. The 3 Sunday in Zion
from the Gospel John 10.11-16. Baptised 2 children.
The 4 Sunday in Salem from John 10.27 baptised 4
children. Wednesday 28 Buried Saml Shealys daughter
& preached from Rom 5.12. Thursday 29 buried old Mrs.
Amick & preached from Rom 8.18. The 1 Sunday in May in
St. Peters from John 10.27 & baptised 1 child. May
27 Married Francis Sharp to Christena Corley.
Saturday the 29 Buried Christian Price & preached from
Ps. 12.1 & baptised 1 child. The 5 Sunday in May
preached in Bethlehem from the gospel John 3.1-15 &
baptised one child.

Page 166: Thursday 3 of June 1857 Buried _____ & preached
from 1 Tim 6.7. The first Sunday in June In St. Peters
from Heb. 10.23 & baptised 3 children. The 2 Sunday
in St. Johns from Heb. 10.23 & baptised 2 children &
in the afternoon from the same in St. Jacobs & baptised 1 child. The 3 Sunday in Zion from Heb. 10.23
& baptised 2 children. The 4 Sunday in Salem from
Heb. 10.23 & in the afternoon from the same in St.
Pauls & baptised 3 children. The 1 Sunday in St.
Peters from the epistle 1 Peter 3.8-15.
The 2 Sunday in July in St. Johns from Mat 5.20
Tuesday 13 buried Adam Eptings son & preached from 2
Tim 1.10.
The 3 Sunday in Zion from the epistle Rom 6.19-23 &
baptised one child. The 4 Sunday in Salem from the
epistle Rom 8. 12-17 & baptised 4 children & in the
afternoon from the same in St. Pauls. Tuesday 27
Buried Wilm Chapman & preached from Gen 3.19.
The first Sunday in August in St. Peters from Luke
16.1-9 & baptised 1 child. Thursday 5 of August Married
John Sulton Esqr to Mary Ann Amick. The 3 Sunday in
Zion from 1 Cor 12.13 & baptised 2 children & in the
afternoon in St. Peters from Luke 18.13 & baptised
2 children. Saturday before the 4 Sunday at old
Mr. Shealys from Luke 18.13 & baptised one child & on
Sunday in Salem from 2 Cor 3.4-11 & baptised 2 children
& in the afternoon in St. Pauls from John 15.5.
Friday 27 of August Buried Fed Gables daughter Mary
Isabel & preached from 2 Cor 5.8.9.
The 5 in Bethlehem from the gospel Luke 10.24-37 &
baptised 1 child. Friday the 3 of Septr Preached a
Thanksgiving Sermon in Zion from Ps 136.1.

Page 167: _____ from the epistle __ 5.16-24 & baptised 2
children & in the afternoon gave Frank Koon the sacrament. Friday 10 Preached a Thanksgiving sermon in
Bethlehem from Ps 95.2 & baptised 1 child. Saturday
11 Buried Wilm Shealys Wife & preached from 2 Cor
5.8.9. & on the same day buried Jacob Fricks daughter
& preached from 2 Cor 5.8.9.
The second Sunday in St. Johns from the epistle Gal.
6.1-10 & in the afternoon in St. Jacobs from the same
& baptised 3 children. The 3 Sunday in Zion from the
epistle Ephes 3.13-21 & baptised 1 child & in the
afternoon in St. Peters from the same & baptised 3
children. Saturday 25 Preached the funeral for Edward
Hare & preached from St. John 5.24 & baptised 1 child
& on the 4 Sunday in Salem from the epistle Ephes 4.1-
6 & in the afternoon in St. Pauls from Ephes 5.8.
Thursday 30 of Septr Buried Frank Koon & preached from
1 Thes 5.9.10.
The first Sunday in Octr in St. Peters from Mat 22.34-
46 & baptised 1 child. The 2 Sunday in St. Johns
from the gospel Mat 9.1-8 & in the afternoon from the
same in St. Jacobs & baptised 1 child. on Monday
11 buried David Koons son & preached from 103 Ps &
13 verse. Tuesday 12 Married John M. Frey to Kezea
Frey. The 3 Sunday in Zion from 2 Cor 4.3.4. & baptised 3 children. Saturday 23 at Adam Shealys from
Ephes 2.1. The 4 Sunday in Salem from Ephes 4.5. &
baptised 8 children & in the afternoon in St. Pauls
from Ephes 2.1. The 5 Sunday in Bethlehem from John

15.5. Tuesday 2 of Novr Buried George Bundrick & preached from 2 Cor 5.8.9.
The 1 Sunday in St. Peters from the epistle Phil 3.17-21 & baptised 5 children. The 2 Sunday in St. John from the epistle Col 1.9-14 & baptised 1 child & in the afternoon from the same in St. Jacobs.

Page 168: The 3 Sunday _____ & in the afternoon from the same in St. Peters. The 4 _____ at Old Mr. Adam Sheal from Heb. 10.23 & on Sunday in Salem from Heb. 4.1 & in the afternoon in St. Pauls from Heb 10.23 & baptised 5 children.
The first Sunday in Decr in St. Peters from Rom 15.23 The 2 Sunday in St. John from Ephes 2.8.9. & baptised 1 child. The 3 Sunday in Zion from Ephes 2.8.9. & in the afternoon from the same in St. Peters.
The 1 Sunday in January 1848 in St. Peters from 1 Peter 4.12-19 & baptised 4 children.
Wednesday 12 Buried Sally Price daughter of Jacob Price & preached from 1 Cor 15.19.
The 3 Sunday in Zion & preached the funeral for David Wilsons wife from 2 Tim 1.10 & baptised one child & in the afternoon in St. Peters from Rom 8.1. The 4 Sunday Buried Elisabeth Setzler & preached from 2 Tim 1.10. Wednesday 26 Buried Lewis Stacks Daughter Martha & preached from John 5.24. The 5 Sunday in Bethlehem from the epistle Rom 13.8-10 & baptised 1 child.
The 1 Sunday in Febry in St. Peters from the gospel Mat 13.24-30 & baptised 4 children. Thursday 10 of Febry Married Wesley Corley to Frances Kleckley. The 2 Sunday in St. Johns from the gospel Mat 17.1-9 & baptised 1 child & in the afternoon from the same in St. Jacobs & baptised 2 children. The 3. Sunday in Febry in Zion from the epistle 1 Cor 9.24-27 & in the afternoon buried Adran Brassels child & preached from 2 Tim 1.10.
The 4 Sunday in Salem from the gospel Luke 3.4-15 & baptised 3 children & in the afternoon from the same in St. Pauls & on Monday I gave Mrs. Kelly the Sacrament.
The first Sunday in March buried Wilm Shulls daughter & preached from 39 Ps 4. The Second Sunday in St. Johns from the epistle 2 Cor 6.1-10 & in the afternoon from the same in St. Jacobs & baptised 3 children. Monday 13 Buried George Kellys Wife & preached from 1 Thes 5.9.10. & baptised 2 children.
   Sunday in Zion from the gospel Mat 15.21-28 & in the afternoon from the same in Peters church.

Page 169: [first few lines very difficult to read]

Monday the 20 of March 1848 Buried Michael Coogles[?] Wife & preached from Job 7.1-__ & on 4 Sunday preached David Risingers[?] funeral from Ps 39 & 4 verse & in the afternoon in St. Paul from _____.
On Wednesday 2- of March buried Capt Jacob Lorick & preached from 1 Cor 15.58-59. Saturday 25 baptised 2 children.
The first Sunday in April in St. Peters from the epistle Gal. 4.21-31 & baptised 2 children.

8 of April Buried John Drafts & preached from
2 Cor 5.6. & baptised 2 children. The 3 Sunday in Zion
from Phil 3.5-11 & baptised 2 children. & in the afternoon from the same in St. Peters
On Goodfriday in Bethlehem from Phil 2.8.
Saturday the 22 a preparatory Sermon in Salem from 1
Cor 11.28 & in the afternoon at Adam Shealys from

III Communicants and in the afternoon at old Mrs
Risingers[?] and baptised 1 child & on Easter Monday
at St Jacobs from 1 Cor 15.17.
The 5 Sunday in Bethlehem from the gospel John 20.19-
21 & baptised 1 child.
The first Sunday in May in St. Peters from the gospel
John 10.11-16 & baptised 4 children. Wednesday 10 of
May buried Henry Klecklys child. The 2 Sunday in St.
John from John 10.11-16 & baptised 1 child & in the
afternoon from the same in St. Jacobs & baptised 2
children. The 3 Sunday in Zion from 1 Cor 10.15-17
Confirmed 9 persons, & administered the Sacrament to
118 & baptised 2 children.
The first day of June being Ascension day in St. Peters
from Acts 1.1-11. Saturday the 3 of June in St. Peters
from 1 Cor 11.28 & Confirmed 40 on the first Sunday in
June preached from 1 Cor 10.15-17 & administered the
Sacrament to 167 & baptised 1 child. The 2 Sunday in
June in St. Johns from the gospel John 14.23-31 &
baptised 1 child in the afternoon from the same in St.
Jacobs & baptised 2 children. Whitsun Monday in Bethlehem from the gospel John 3.10-21. The 3 Sunday in
Zion the Funeral for Saml Slone from 2 Cor 5.8.9. &
baptised 2 children & in the afternoon in St. Peters
from John 3.7 & baptised 1 child. The 4 Sunday in
Salem from Luke 16.19-31 & baptised 2 children & in
the afternoon from the same in St. Pauls & baptised

15-17 Confirmed 4 & administered the Sacrament to
The 2 Sunday in July in St. Johns from Luke 15.1-10 &
in the afternoon from the same in St. Jacobs & baptised
one child. The 3 Sunday in Zion from John 10.27 &
baptised one child. Tuesday the 18 buried Adam Hips
daughter & preached from 2 Cor 5.8.9. The 4 Sunday in
Salem from 1 Peter 3.4-15 & in the afternoon St. Paul
from 1 Peter 3.15 & on Monday 24 buried George Wessinger & preached from 39 Ps 4 verse.

Page 170: The 5 Sunday in July 1848 I preached in Bethlehem the
Funeral for Samuel Boney from Rom 6.23.
The first in August in St. Peters from the epistle
Rom 6.19-23 & in the afternoon at old Mr. Balentines
from 1 Cor 15.2 & baptised 1 child. The 2 Sunday in
St. John from the epistle Rom 8.12-17 & in the after-
noon from the same in St. Jacobs & baptised 1 child.
The 3 Sunday in Zion from Rom 8 & 12 verse & the 17
in the afternoon from _____ & baptised 1 child.
Saturday 19 Buried John Lewis & preached from Heb 2.6.
Saturday 26 Preached at old Mr. Shealys from 1 Cor 15.
2 & baptised 1 child. Sunday 27 in Salem from Rom 8.
12-17 & baptised 1 child & in the afternoon from the
same in St. Pauls & baptised 1 child.
The first Sunday in Septr 1848 in St. Peters from
the gospel Luke 18.9-14 & baptised 1 child & in the
afternoon at old Mr. Balentines from John 8.31.

Wednesday 6 Buried John Freys Wife & preached from
1 Tim 4.8. Sept 12 Buried Kings daughter & preached
from Col 3.4. The 2 Sunday in St. Johns from the
Epistle 2 Cor 3.4-11 & in the afternoon from the same
in St. Jacobs & baptised 1 child. The 3 Sunday in
Zion from the gospel Luke 10.23-37 & in the afternoon
from the same. Saturday 23 P at old Adam Shealys from
John 10.15 & baptised 3 children. The 4 Sunday in
Salem from John 10.15 & in the afternoon in St. Pauls
from 1 Peter 2.25 & baptised 1 child. Thursday 2
buried John Geiger & P from Col 3.4. & baptised 1
child. Saturday 30 buried Adam Eptings child & preached
from Col 3.4..
Sunday the 1 of October buried old Mrs. Loner &
preached from John 5.25 & in the afternoon at old Mr.
Balentines from Heb 4.1 Septr 15 Buried George Mayes
wife & preached from Col 3.4. The 2 Sunday in St.
John from the gospel Luke 7.11-17 & baptised 3 children
& in the afternoon from the same in St. Jacobs. The
3 Sunday in Zion from Heb 4.1 & baptised 1 child & in
the afternoon from the same in St. Peters. Tuesday
17 the Rev. Mr. Fox preached in Zion & I married John
Wilson to Harriet Seastrunk. On Saturday the 21
Preached at old Mr. Shealys from Heb. 4.1 & baptised
1 child. The 4 Sunday in Salem from the gospel Mat
22.34-46 & baptised 1 child. The 5 Sunday in Bethlehem the Rev. Mr. Fox preached & I baptised 1 child
The 1 Sunday in Novr the Rev. Mr. Fox preached in St.
Peters & I baptised one child. The second Sunday I
was prevented by sickness & disagreeable weather. The
3 Sunday in Zion   & baptised 1 child. The 4 Sunday
buried Jacob Huffman & preached from Job 14.1.2. The
first Sunday in Decr in St. Peters from Rom 13.11-14
The 2 Sunday in St. John, Rom 15.13. Wednesday 12 buried Elias Taylers wife & baptised 2 children John 5.25.
The 3 Sunday in Zion from 1 Cor 4.1 & baptised 2 children & in the afternoon from the same in St. Pauls &
baptised 2 children. Christmas day in Bethlehem from
Luke 2.10. Friday 29 buried George Likes wife &
preached from John 5.25. The 5 Sunday in Bethlehem
Gal. 4.6.

Page 171: Monday 8 of January 1849 Buried George Monts son &
preached from Marck 10.14. The 4 of January married
Levi Wheeler to T. C. Fikes. The first Sunday in
St. Peters from the epistle Rom 12.1-6 & baptised 2
children. The Second Sunday in St. Peters from the
epistle Rom 12.6-16 & in the afternoon in St. Pauls
from the same and baptised 2 children.
Tuesday 16 buried Joseph Bolands child & Mark 10.14.
The 3 Sunday in Zion from the gospel Mat 8.13 & baptised 1 child & in the afternoon from the same in St.
Peters & baptised 1 child.
Monday 22 1849 W. Amick commenst working. The 4 Sunday
in Salem from Mat 8.23-27 & baptised 3 children & in
the afternoon from the same in St. Pauls & baptised
2 children.
Monday 29 Buried Meltons wife & preached from 2 Tim
1.10. The first Sunday in February in St. Peters from
Mat 13.24-30 & baptised 1 child & in the afternoon
preached the funeral for M. Lindsey from 1 Cor 15.56
On Thursday the 8 buried Emily Jackson & preached
from 1 Cor 15.56 & in the afternoon buried Joseph

Bolands wife & preached from Col 3.4. The 3 Sunday in Zion from the gospel Luke 18.31-43. The 4 Sunday in Salem from Mat 4.1-11 & in the afternoon from the same in St. Paul & baptised 1 child. The first Sunday in March 1849 in St. Peters from the gospel Mat 15.21-28. The 8 of March Married Jesse Derrick to Mary Ann Coogler. The 2 Sunday in St. Johns from Ephes 5.1-13 & in the afternoon from the same in St. Jacobs & baptised 3 children. The 3 Sunday in Zion from the epistle Gal. 4.28 & baptised 3 children. The 4 Sunday in March in Salem from the gospel John 8.46-59 & in the afternoon from the same in St. Paul. The first Sunday in April in St. Peters from the epistle Phil 2.5-11 & baptised 1 child.
Goodfriday in Bethlehem from Isa 53 & baptised 1 child. Easter Sunday in Zion from Mat 26.26-28 & administered the Sacrament to 103 Comt & Confirmed 4.
Easter Monday in Salem from Luke 24.13-35 & baptised 6 children & on the afternoon from the same in St. Pauls. Thursday 12 Buried Adam Shealys wife & preached from John 5.25 & baptised 1 child. Saturday 14 buried Joseph Earharts Wife & preached from John 5.25. The 3 Sunday in St. Pauls from Mat 26.26-28 & administered the Sacrament. Tuesday 17 Married George Mayer to Anna Barbara Derrick. Friday 20 Buried John Stoutemyer & preached from John 6.47. The 4 Sunday in St. John & preached Adam Bundricks funeral from John 5. 25 & baptised 4 children & in the afternoon in St. Jacobs from the gospel John 10.11-16 & baptised 2 children. Friday 27 Buried Danl Kleckleys wife & preached from Eph

Page 172: Sermons 2505

Baptisms 2225

Confirmants 968
Marriages (?) 288

Ordinates 2

Page 173: Blank

Page 174: The 5 Sunday in April 1849 administered the Sacrament in Bethlehem Church to 24 Communicants & preached from John 6.68 & baptised 2 children.
The 1 Sunday in May preached in St. Peters or Meetzes Church from Rom 10.1 & baptised 1 child & in the afternoon In Zion from Rom 10.1
Friday 11 of May Buried Adam Metz & preached from Col 3.2-4. Saturday 12 Preached in St. Johns Church from 1 Cor 11.28 & on Sunday from Mat 26. 26-28 & administered the sacrament of the Lords Supper. Sunday afternoon buried George Fulmers Wife & preached from John 5.24 & baptised 1 child.
The 4 in Salem Confirmed 26 & administered the Sacrament to 132 Comts. & baptised 10 children. The 1 Sunday in June in St. Peters from 1 Cor 11.23-26 & baptised 3 children & Confirmed 24 & administered the Sacrament **to 206**. The 2 Sunday in Meetzes Church from 1 Cor 11.23-26 & baptised 1 child. Buried John Fricks child on Friday 15 of June & preached from Mark 10.14.

The 3 Sunday in Zion from St. John 3.36 & baptised 1
child & in the afternoon from the same in St. Peters
The 4 in Salem from John 3.36 & in the afternoon in
St. Paul from Luke 15.2. The first Sunday in July
1849 in St. Peters from St. John 3.36. Friday the 6
Buried John Cooglers Wife & preached from John 11.25
The 2 Sunday in St. John 3.36 & in the afternoon from
the same in St. Jacobs & baptised 1 child. The 3
Sunday in Zion from Rom 6.3-11 & baptised 2 children
& in the afternoon from the same in St. Peters. The
5 Sunday in Bethlehem from the gospel Mat 7.15-23 &
baptised 1 child. The first Sunday in August Married
the widow Earigle to Henry Shwartz (sic) in St. Peters
piney wood from the gospel Luke 16.1-9 & baptised 1
child & in the afternoon in Zion the funeral for
Jacob Kooks child from rom 5.18 & baptised 3 children.
The 2 Sunday in St. John from Titus 3.5-7 & in the afternoon from the same in St. Jacobs & baptised 2 children. The 3 Sunday in August in Zion preached John Buffs
funeral from Luke 12.37-38 & in the afternoon in St.
Peters from Luke 18.9-14. Monday 20 buried Nathaniel
Hermans child & preached from 2 Tim 1.10. Saturday 25
Buried George Keisler & preached from 1 Cor 15.56. The
4 Sunday in Salem from the epistle 2 Cor 3.4-11 &
baptised 7 children & in the afternoon from the same
in St. Pauls & baptised 2 children. The first Sunday
in St. Peters from the gospel Luke 10.23-37 & baptised
Fricks child & preached from Rom 5.18.
Thursday 6 of Septr Married Adam Younginer to Sarah
Gable.

Page 175:   Friday 7 of Septr 1849 buried Catharine Gartman &
preached from Rom 5.18. The 2 Sunday in St. John from
the epistle Gal. 5.16-24 & baptised 1 child & from
the same in the afternoon in St. Jacobs. The 3 Sunday
in Zion from the gospel Mat 6.24-34 & in the afternoon
from the same in St. Peters.
Monday 17 buried George Leapharts wife.
The 4 Sunday in Salem from Rom 10.1 & baptised 2
children & in the afternoon from the same in St. Paul
Friday 28 of Septr preached a Thanksgiving Sermon
in Zion from 1 Chron 16.34.
The 5 Sunday at Broad River from Rom 10.1 & baptised 1
child.
The 1 Sunday in St. Peters from 1 Cor 1.4-9 & baptised
1 child. The 2 Sunday in St. John from Mat 9.1-8 &
in the afternoon from the same in St. Jacob. Tuesday
the 16 Buried Martin Sox's son & preached from 1 Thes
5.9
Saturday 30 October buried Elisabeth Whites & preached
from 1 Thes 5.9. The 4 Sunday in Salem from the gospel
St. John 4.47-54 & baptised 2 children & in the afternoon from the same in St. Paul. Thursday the 1 of
Novr 1849 Buried Thomas Burkit & preached from Rom
5.18 & in the afternoon buried Lewis Stacks Daughter
Friday 2 of Novr buried Lewis Stack & preached from
1 Thes 5.9.
The first Sunday in St. Peters from the gospel Mat
18.23-35 & baptised 2 children.
The 2 Sunday in St. John from Phil 3.17-21 & baptised
2 children. The 3 Sunday in Zion from Col 1.13.14 &
in the afternoon from the same in St. Peters. The
4 Sunday Married Saml Fulmore to Mary Ann Bowers &

then preached the funeral for old Mrs. Vansant in
Salem Church from 1 Thes 4.13-18 & baptised 1 child
& in the afternoon in St. Paul from 1 John 3.1.
The first Sunday in December 1849 in St. Peters from
the epistle Rom 13.11-14. Wednesday 5 Buried David
Epting & preached from St John 5.24 & on Thursday the
6 Married Solomon Shealy to Miney Derrick & baptised
2 children. The 2 Sunday in St. John from 2 Peter
3.1 & baptised 1 child & in the afternoon from the
same in St. Jacobs. Tuesday the 11 Married Jefferson
Sea to Polly Amick & baptised 1 child. The 3 Sunday
in Decr in Zion from 2 Peter 3.1 & married Elijah
Wingard & Caroline Gable & in the afternoon from the
same in St. Peters. Thursday 31 buried old Mrs. Aull
& preached from Col 3.4. The 4 Sunday in Salem from
2 Peter 3.1 & Married John Long to Miley Price & in
the afternoon in St. Pauls from 2 Peter 3.1.
Cristmas (sic) day preached in Bethlehem from the
gospel & baptised 1 child.

Page 176: Saturday 29 of Decr 1849 Buried Willm. Leavers Son &
preached from 1 Cor 15.57
Sunday 30 preached in Bethlehem from 2 Peter 3.1 &
baptised 1 child.
January 3 Thursday Married Richard Hindrex & Eliza-
beth Drafts & baptised 1 child. The first Sunday in
January 1850 married Joseph Boland to Elisabeth Harriet
Shealy & then preached in St. Peters from Mat 2.1-12
The 2 Sunday in St. John & preached Martin Setzlers
Funeral from 2. Cor 5.1 & baptised 1 child & on Monday
Buried Henry Bone & preached from 1 John 3.14. The
3 Sunday in Zion from Gal. 6.14 & baptised 1 child &
in the afternoon from the same in St. Peters.
The 4 Sunday in Salem from the epistle 1 Cor 9.27 &
in the afternoon in St. Paul from Heb .0.23 & baptised
1 child. The first Sunday in Febry 1850 in St. Peters
from the gospel Luke 8.4-15 & baptised 1 child. Tuesday
12 Married Elliot Gant & Ann E. Veal.
Saturday 16 buried Gasper Ellisor & preached from 1
John 3.14. The 3 Sunday in Zion from the gospel Mat
4.1-11 & baptised 1 child & in the afternoon from the
same in St. Peters. Thursday 21 Married Jacob Hellebran to Polly Addy. The 4 Sunday in Salem from the
gospel Mat 15.24-28 & in the afternoon from the same
in St. Paul. The first Sunday in March in St. Peters
from the epistle Ephes 5.1-13 & baptised 1 child.
The second Sunday in St. John from Gal. 3.22 & in
the afternoon from the same in St. Jacobs & baptised
one child. Saturday 9 of March Buried Dr. G. Koon &
preached from 1 Tim 6.6-8. The 3 Sunday prevented on
account of high water. The 4 Sunday in Salem from
the epistle Phil 2.5-11 & in the afternoon from the
same in St. Paul & baptised 1 child.
Goodfriday 29 Preach in Bethlehem from Phil 2.8.
Easter preached in Bethlehem from Rom 4.25 & baptised
6 children. Easter Monday preached in St. Jacob
from Rom 4.25. The first Sunday in April 1850 preached
in St. Peters from Rom 4.25 & baptised 4 children. The
2 Sunday in St Jacob from St. John 10.11-16 & baptised
4 children. The 3 Sunday in Zion from John 10.11-16
& baptised 2 children & in the afternoon in St. Peters
& preached a funeral Sermon for Mountain Seas Son from

1 Tim 6.7.8. The 4 Sunday in April in Salem from John 10.11-16 & baptised 3 children & in the afternoon in Pauls church & preached the funeral for old Mrs. Craps from 1 Tim 6.6-8.

Page 177: Tuesday 30 of April Buried Polly Miller & preached from 1 Tim 6.6-8. Thursday the 2 of May 1850 Buried Henry Addy & preached from Job 19.25-27. Saturday the 4 of May in St. Peters from Prov. 16.1 & baptised 1 child & 9 blacks.
The first Sunday from Mat 26.2-28 Confirmed 20 & Administered the Sacrament to 197. The 2 Sunday in St. Johns from Heb 2.3. & baptised 3 children & in the afternoon from the same at George Amicks a funeral Sermon for his son Daniel. Saturday the 18 in Zion from Prov 16.1 & baptised 4 children on the 3 Sunday being Whit Sunday preached from Mark 14.22-25 Confirmed 6 & administered the Sacrament to 104 persons. Whitson Monday in St. Peters pineywood from the gospel St. John 3.16-21 & baptised 1 child. The 4 Sunday in May in Salem from Mat 26.26-29 Confirmed 18 & administered the Sacrament to 142 persons. On Saturday before the 4 Sunday in Salem preached from Prov 16.1 & baptised 3 adults & one child in the afternoon in St. Pauls from Luke 16.29 & baptised 1 child.
The first Sunday in June 1850 in Bethlehem & administered the Sacrament & baptised 1 child & Confirmed one person.
The Saturday before the Second Sunday in St. Jacobs from Prov 16.1 & on the 2 Sunday preached from 1 Cor 11.23-26 & Confirmed 10 Persons & administered the Sacrament to 45. The 3 Sunday in Zion from the gospel Luke 15.1-10 & baptised 1 child & on Monday the 17 preached the funeral for Mrs. Williams from John 5.25. The 4 Sunday in Salem from Isa 53.6 & baptised 3 children & in the afternoon in St. Paul from 1 Peter 2.24. The 5 Sunday in Bethlehem from Gal. 4. 28 & baptised 3 children. The 4 of July Married Wilm. Rish to Martha Ann Cannon. The first Sunday in July 1850 in St. Peters from the gospel Mat 5.21-2-. & baptised 2 children. The 2 Sunday in St. Johns from the epistle Rom 6.19-23 & in the afternoon from the same in St. Jacobs. Friday 19 buried John Martin & preached from John 11.25.36. The 3 Sunday in Zion from the gospel Mat 7.15-23 & in the afternoooon from the same in St. Peters & baptised 2 children. The 4 Sunday in Salem from the gospel Luke 16.1-9 & baptised 4 children & in the afternoon from the same in St. Paul & baptised 1 child & on Monday baptised 2 of John Gables children. Friday 2 of August buried Daniel Prices child & preached from Col 3.4. & baptised 1 child.
The 1 Sunday in August 1850 preached in St. Peters from 1 Cor 1.18 & baptised 1 child. The 2 Sunday in August buried John Franklow & preached from John 11.25. The 3 Sunday in Zion from the epistle 2 Cor 3.4-11

Page 178: & baptised 1 child & in the afternoon from the same in St. Peters. Tuesday 20 of August buried Daniel Cromers child & preached from Luke 18.16. The 4 Sunday in Salem from the Gospel Luke 10.23-37 & baptised 1 child & in the afternoon from the same in St. Paul. The first Sunday in St. Peters from the epistle Gal. 5.16-24 &

baptised 1 child. The __ Sunday in St. John from Titus 3.5. & baptised 1 child & in the afternoon from the same in St. Jacobs. Thursday 19 Buried Christian Frick & preached from 2 Tim 1.10. Saturday 21 preached the funeral for William Shealys child from 2 Tim 1.10 & baptised 2 children. The 4 Sunday in Salem church from Titus 3.5 & baptised 1 child & in the afternoon from the same in St. Paul & baptised 1 child. The 5 Sunday Buried Jacob Dericks son & preached from 2 Tim 1.10 & baptised 1 child. The first Sunday in October in St. Peters or piney wood from the gospel Mat 9.1-8 & baptised 2 children in the afternoon Buried David Mccartys child & preached from John 6.47. The 2 Sunday in St. Jacobs (?) from the gospel Mat 22.1-14 & baptised 2 children. Tuesday the 15 married Ervin Baughnight & Barbara Ann Metz. The 3 Sunday in Zion from the gospel John 4.47-54 & in the afternoon from the same in St. Peters & baptised 2 children. Wednesday 23 buried Christian Freshley & preached from St. John 6.47. & on Thursday the 24 being the day appointed by the Governor I preached in Bethlehem from the 50 Ps 14.15 verses. The 4 Sunday in Salem from the 5o Ps 14.15 verses & baptised 2 children. The 1 Sunday in Novr Married Osro Boland & Levina Koon & then preached in St. Peters or piney wood Church from the gospel Mat 22.5-22 & baptised 1 child Tuesday the 5 of November Buried Henry Wingard & preached from St. John 6.47 & baptised 3 children. The 2 Sunday in St. John from the gospel Mat 9.18-26 & in the afternoon from the same in St. Jacobs. Tuesday 12 Married Joel W. Harman & Mariah A. Franklow. The 3 Sunday in Zion from 1 Cor 3.11 & baptised 1 child & in the afternoon from the same in St. Peters. The 4 Sunday in Salem from 2 Peter 3.3-14 & in the afternoon from 2 Peter 3.1.
Thursday 28 Married John Frances Summer to Polley Addy The first Sunday in Decr 1850 in St. Peters or piney wood Church preached from Col 1.15. The 2 Sunday from the same in St. Jacobs & on Wednesday 11 Buried Henry Earigles child & preached from St. John 6.47. The 3 Sunday in Zion from Col 1.15 & in the afternoon from the same in St. Peter on Tuesday the 17 Buried Joseph Bolands child & preached from 1 Thes 4.18.
The 4 Sunday in Decr in Salem from Col 1.15 & in the afternoon from the same in St. Paul
on Monday 23 baptised Jefferson Hooks child. Christmas preached in Bethlehem from Mat 1.21 & on Tuesday the 31 buried old Wilm Balentine & preached from Heb 9.27
The first Sunday in January 1851 preached in St. Peters from Titus 3.4-7 & baptised 1 child. The 2 Sunday in St John from the epistle Rom 12.1-6 & in the
afternoon from the same in St. Jacobs & baptised 1 child. The 3 Sunday in Zion from Rom 12.1-6 & baptised 1 child. The 4 Sunday in Salem from Rom 13.4.5. & baptised 1 child & in the afternoon in St. Pauls from 1 Cor 12.13 & baptised 1 child.
Thursday the 30 of January 1851 Married Henry Koon & Caroline Sultan & baptised one child & in the afternoon Married Elias Sease & Elijeana Lewe (?). The first Sunday in Febry preached in St. Peters (or piney woods) from Ecclesiastes 7.16.17 & baptised 1 child & in the afternoon buried Henry Hendrixes child & preached

from 1 Thes 5.9. The second Sunday in St. Jacobs Church from the gospel Mat 13.24-30 & baptised 4 children. The 3 Sunday prevented from preaching on account of high water. Thursday 20 of Febry Married Wiley Shealy & Mary Marthaann Halman. The 4 Sunday preached in Salem from ecle 7.16.17 & baptised 2 children & from the same in the afternoon in St. Paul & baptised 1 child.

Tuesday the 25 of Febry 1851 Married Jacob David Son to one of Jacobs Amicks Daughters. The first Sunday in March 1851 preached in St. Peters from the gospel Luke 18.31-43 & baptised 2 children. The 2 Sunday in March in St. Johns from the Epistle 2 Cor 6.1-10 & in the afternoon from the same in St. Peters & baptised 1 child. The 4 Sunday in Salem & Rev. D. Efird preached from Jer 8.22 & in the afternoon he preached in St. Paul from St. John 3.16 & I baptised 2 children. The 5 Sunday in March Married John Coogler to Susanna Younginer & then preached Bethlehem from 2 Cor 6.1 & baptised Daniel Metzes Wife & his grand child. The 1 Sunday in April 1851 preached in pineywoods church from the gospel John 8.46-59 & baptised 3 children. Tuesday 8 Married Robert Gartman to Rachel Franklow The 2 Sunday in April in St. Jacobs from Rom 5.1 Goodfriday in Bethlehem from the 1 Peter 3.18. Saturday 19 in Zion from 2 Cor 13.5.

Easter Sunday in Zion from 1 Cor 10.15.16 Confirmed 6 & 120 Comts. & baptised 1 child.

Wednesday 23 buried old Adam Shealy & preached from Heb 9.27. The 4 Sunday in April in Salem from the same in St. Pauls. The first Sunday in May in St. Peters from the gospel John 10.11-16 & baptised 3 children. Thursday 8 Buried old Adam Amick & preached from Job 7.

The 2 Sunday in May in St. Johns from John 21.15-17 & baptised 3 children & in the afternoon from the same in St. Paul & baptised 3 children.

The 3 Sunday in Zion from the epistle James 1.16-21 & in the afternoon from the same in St. Peters & baptised 1 child. Friday 23 buried Billy Seas child & preached from Luke 18.16 & baptised 2 children.

The 4 Sunday in Salem from the epistle James 1.22-37 & baptised 1 child & in the afternoon from the same in St. Paul & baptised 1 child.

Saturday 31 Preached in St. Peters from 2 Cor 13.5 & baptised 1 child.

Page 180: Saturday 31 of May 1851 Preached at Mrs. Bolands from Rom 8.18. Sunday the first of June in St. Peters or piney wood from 1 Cor 10.15.16. Confirmed 1 & administered the Sacrament to 180 Communicants. Saturday 7 of June preached in St. Jacobs from 1 Cor 11.28 & on Whit Sunday in St. Jacobs from 1 Cor 10.15.16 Confirmed 4 & administered the Sacrament to 47. The 3 Sunday in Zion from the gospel St. John 3.1-15 & in the afternoon from the same in St. Peters. Thursday 5 of June Married Saml Bookman to Harriet McCan. Wednesday 18 buried Joel Corleys child & preached from Luke 18.16 The 4 Sunday in Salem from Heb. 2.3. & baptised 2 children & in the afternoon from the same in St. Paul & baptised 1 child. The 5 Sunday in June in Bethlehem church from Luke 15.1.2. & baptised 3 children. July 5 buried J. Millers wife & preached

from Rom 5.12 & baptised 1 child.
The 1 Sunday in July in St. Peters from the gospel
Luke 15.1-10 & baptised 1 child & on Monday 7
7 buried Robert Sultons child & preached from Luke
18.16. The 2 Sunday in St. John from Luke 15.1.2.
& baptised 2 children & in the afternoon from the same
in St. Jacob. The 3 Sunday in Zion from the epistle
1 Peter 3.8-15 & in the afternoon from the same in
St. Peters & baptised 1 child. The 4 Sunday in Salem
from the gospel Mat 5.20-26 & in the afternoon preached
the funeral for Daniel Lominick from 1 Cor 15.55 &
baptised 2 children. The 1 Sunday in August in St.
Peters from the epistle Rom 6.19-23 Tuesday the 5 of
August married Saml Lever to Margaret Burket.
The 2 Sunday in St. Jacobs Church from the gospel Mat
7.15-23 & baptised 1 child & in the afternoon buried
John Chapmans daughter & preached from 1 Cor 15.55 &
baptised 2 children. The 3 Sunday in Zion from the
gospel Luke 16.1-9 & baptised 1 child & in the afternoon from the same in St. Peters. The 4 Sunday buried
Michael Drafts D. & preached from Rev. 14.13. The 5
Sunday in Bethlehem from Romans 10.1 & baptised 2
children. The first Sunday in Septr Married John Henry
Amick to Ellen Ham after which I preached in St. Peters
from Rom 10.1 & baptised 5 children.
Wednesday 10 buried Jacob Bundricks daughter & preached
from Rev 14.13. Saturday 13 buried Solomon Addy &
preached from John 11.25. The 2 Sunday in St. Johns
from Gal 3.15-22 & in the afternoon from the same in
St. Jacobs & baptised 3 children on Tuesday 16 buried
Franklin Addy & preached from 2 Tim 1.10. The 3 Sunday
in Zion from the epistle Gal. 5.16-24 & in the afternoon from the same in St. Peters on Tuesday 23 buried
Jacob Kinslers child & preached from 2 Tim 1.10. The
4 Sunday in Salem church from Rom 10.1 & baptised 2
children & in the afternoon from the same in St. Paul
& baptised 2 children.

END

Academy 13
Addy, Adah 30
    Franklin 81
    George, sons of 24
    Mrs. George 69
    Henry 78
    Hirem 68
    Miss 51
    Polley 79
    Polly 77
    Simion, child of 30
    Simon, child of 52
    Solomon 81
    Squer 49
Alewin, Philip, child of 53
Aleywine, Philip, child of 63
Amick, Adam 80
    Adam, dau. of 66
    Daniel 78
    Mrs. Daniel 25
    David, dau. of 69
    Mrs. Gasper 38
    George 78
    Henry, child of 52
    Jacob, dau of 80
        son of 58
    John Henry 81
    Mary Ann 38, 71
    Mrs. 63, 69, 70
    Polly 77
    Sarah 57
    W. 74
Aull, Harman 35
    Mrs. 77
Austen, Elizabeth 7
Auston, Eliza 35

Bachman's (Rev.) church 17
Bailey, John, child of 50
Baity, John, child of 68
Balentine, James dau of 58
    Mr. 73(2), 74
    Wilm 79
  see also Ballentine
Bales, Mrs. 32
Ballentine, George 61
    Sally 70
  see also Balentine
Barefield, ____ 43
Bates, Col., son of 24
    Jacob, daus of 36
Baty, John, child of 46
Baty, ____ child of 50
Baughnight, Ewin 79
Bauknight, Margaret Elisabeth 67
Bayle, Squire 33
Bealem (?), the Rev. 10
Beaty, Mariah 14
Belen, Rev. 11
Bell, John 67
    John, child of 22, 70
Bendenbaugh, ____ 37

Bernart, Polly 2
Bernhardt, Luesia 34
Bethel Church 2, 31
Bethlehem Church 1(3), 3(2),
  8, 11, 13, 14(2), 15,
  16(3), 17, 18(4), 19(5),
  20(3), 21(4), 22(4),
  23(5), 24, 25(2), 26(4),
  27, 28, 29, 32(3), 33(3),
  34(3), 35(3), 37, 38(2),
  39, 40(3), 41(2), 42(2),
  43, 44(2), 45(2), 46(4),
  47, 48(4), 49(2), 50(2),
  51(2), 52, 53(2), 54(2),
  55(4), 56(2), 57(2), 58(2),
  59(3), 60, 61, 62, 64(2),
  65, 66(2), 67(3), 68(3),
  69(2), 70(2), 71(3), 72,
  73(4), 74(3), 75(2), 76,
  77(4), 78(2), 79(2), 80(3),
  81

Bethlehem Church (Broad River)
  2(2), 3(2), 4(2), 5(2), 6,
  7(4), 8, 9(2), 10(4), 11,
  12(2), 13, 15, 17(2), 31(2),
  32(3), 33, 36, 37, 45, 49,
  76

Bethlehem Church (Newberry)
  1(2), 3(4), 4(3), 5(5),
  6(7), 8(2), 12, 25, 27

Beyer, Mrs. Samuel 33
Bezoon, Elisa 14
Bickely, Jacob 6
Bickley, Mrs. 59
    Richard 67
    West, child of 51
Bickly(?), James Allen 65
    Mrs. 52
Black(?), Mary 5
Boland, Abraham 38
    Adam 39
    Catharine 44
    Ephraim Walter 64
    John Middleton 68
    Joseph 77
    Joseph, child of, 48(2),
      74, 79
    Mrs. Joseph 75
    Levi 64
    Mrs. 80
    Osro 79
Bone, Henry 77
    Miss 4
Boney, Fanney 47
    Jany 60
    Samuel 73
Book, Selena 36
Bookman, Anna 19
    Daniel 28

Bookman, David 67
         John 5
         Joseph 68
         Mrs. 17
         Mrs. child of 17
         Samuel 43, 80
         Thoams 43
         Thomas, son of 40
         Widow 14
Bookman, ____ child of 8
Boozer, David, child of 3
         Widow 2
Bough, Mrs. 4
Bouknight, Amelia 42
         Christenah P. 8
         Daniel 19, 35
         George, son of 48
         Henry 14
         Jessee 19
         Joanna 62
         Joel 23
         John 8, 18
       \ Mrs. John 17
         John Junr 65
         Mary 67
         Mr. 37
         Mrs. 25
         Samuel 21
         Thomas 59, 64
         Mrs. Thomas 62
Bowers, George Washington 49
         Margaret 42
         Mary Ann 76
         Polly 41
         Sally, child of 62
         Stephen 60
         Susanna 64
         ____ 31
Branham, William C. 22
Brassel, Adran, child of 72
Brassell, Aaron 70
         Mrs. 47
Bright, John 16, 36
         Polly 55
Brown, Rev. Abel John 40(3),
   42(2), 43(2), 45(3),
   51(3), 55(5)
Bryson, Henry 64
         Widow 60
Buff, John 35, 76
         ____ 33
Bundrick, Adam 75
         George 72
         Mrs. George 63
         Jacob 66
         Jacob, dau. of 81

Bundrick, Mrs. dau of 66
Burge, Elender 2
Burket, Margaret 81
Burkit, Thomas 76
Buzzard, Peter 27
Byers, Samuel 32

Calk, James Hillard 49
Cannon, Col. 6
         Martha Ann 78
Carr, James 59
Caughman, Jacob 24
         Mrs. Jacob 21
         Martin 26
         Mrs. 17
Caughman's church 7
Cauley, Juda 29
Chalmers, Henry 29
Chapman, Adam 29
         Caroline 44
         David 57
         David, dau. of 54
         Mrs. David, dau of 61
         George 66
         John, dau of 81
         Mrs. John 30
         Mrs., dau of 63
         William 44, 71
Chupp, Bity 36
Chupps, Sarah 43
Clapp, David, dau of 66
Clark, Polly 23
Comalander, Alexander, child of 66
         Caty 8
         George, child of 47
         John 3
Coogle, Daniel 1
         David 11
         Mathias 1
         Mrs. Michael(?) 72
         Mrs. 4
         Sarah 19
Coogler, ____ 48
         Catharine 63
         David 62
         Jesse 41
         John 80
         Mrs. John 76
         Mary 21
         Mary Ann 75
         Mathias 2
         Mathias, child of 50
              son of 25
         Panilipy 58
         Mrs. Uriah 54
Cook, Rev. 18

Corley, Christena 70
    Daniel 22, 60
    Emanuel, child of 18
    Jesse 50
    Joel 29
    Joel, child of 80
    John 64
    John, son of 11
    Michael 41
    Michael, child of 67
    Noah 58
    Rebeckah 1
    Reubin 61
    Samuel 47
    Sarah 37
    Wesley 72
Coughman, Martin 10
    West, child of 2
Counts, Mrs. John 30
    Nancy 19
    ___ child of 6, 25
Countze, Col., child of 6
Crapps, George 70
Craps, David, son of 61
    Elisa 68
    Henry 30
    John, child of 46
    Michael, child of 4
    Mrs. 78
    Nancy 39
Crate, Rebeckah 15
Crim, Jacob 65
Cromer, Andrew 46
    Daniel 58
    Daniel, child of 78
    David 38
    Sarah 31
Crout, Azariah 45
    Mrs. Azariah 48
    Lewis 64
    Reuben 68
    Uriah 57
    Uriah, child of 66

Danner, Mr. 66(3), 67
Davis, Drury, son of 54
    Mr. 68
Dent, Elizabeth 11
    Nancy 3
Derick, Barbara 8
    Elizabeth 24
    Jacob, child of 14
        son of 79
    John 13
    John, child of 13
    Martha Ann Elisabeth 64
    Sally 28(2)
Derrick, Capt. Andrew 12
    Anna Barbara 75
    Jesse 75
    Miney 77
Dominick, Henry 45
Donner, Mr. 66

Draft, Daniel, dau of 21
Drafts, Ann 58
    Barbara 26
    Mrs. Daniel 68
    Elizabeth 77
    George 57
    Jessee 46
    John 73
    Michael 30, 64, 81
    Michael, dau of 51
Dreher, Jesse 14, 27
Derhers, Mrs. George 14
    J. J. 23
Drehr, Barbara 14
    David 1
    Nancy 35
Dubart, Mary 2
    Philip 2
Dupryee, Mary Ann 2

Eaffie, child of 47, 56
Earhart, Adam 66
    Jacob, dau of 33
    John, dau of 15
    John P. 58
    Joseph, dau of 47
    Mrs. Joseph 75
    Mrs. 16
    Nancy Julia 64
Earigle, Artimas 65
    Catherine Margaret 39
    David 39
    Elisabeth 58
    Eve 57
    Eve Margaret 38
    Henry 40
    Henry, child of 79
        son of 58
        dau of 56
    Jacob 39, 57, 59
    John, children of 36
    Kesiah 49
    Mary Barbara 41
    Mrs. 65
    Nancy 60
    Sally 48, 70
    Widow 76
Effler, Miss 17
    Sarah 12
Efird, Rev. D. 80
Efie, child of 47, 56
Egner's church (Newberry) 28
Eiglebarger, George, child of 6
    John 1
    Luesia 28
    Mary 11
Eleazer, Henry 5
Eliaser, George, son of 69
Eliser, Elizabeth 18
    John 68(2)
    John, son of 38
Ellenbarg, Caroline 35
Elliser(?), Caty Gibson 44

Elliser, John 44
    Mary Ann 49
Ellisor, Gasper 77
Epting, Adam 46
    Adam, child of 38, 74
        son of 71
    David 77
    Elisabeth 50
    George 70
    George, children of 61
    Mrs. George 32
    Jacob 6
    Widow 59
    William, child of 54
Erigle, Jacob dau. of 41
Eve, Mrs. Win 64
Evins, Mrs. 55

Fike, David, son of 58
    Martin 63, 65
    Mrs. 70
Fikes, Martha Elisabeth 65
    T. C. 74
Floid, Miss, child of 24
Fox, Mrs. John 22
    Rev. Mr. 74(3)
    ____ child of 22
Fraisher, William 51
Francklow, John 51
    Rev. 2
Franklow, Father 12(2)
    Jane Caroline 58
    John 78
    Mariah A. 79
    Mrs. 52
    Rachel 80
    Rev. 10
Frats, Elisabeth Jane 48
Frayser, Emeline Elisabeth 63
Freshley, Christian 79
Freshly, Eli, child of 54
Frey, Abraham 19
    Abraham, dau. of 37
    George, child of 4
    John 8, 19
    Mrs. John 15, 74
    John M. 71
    Kezea 71
    Mr. 28
    Mrs. 28
Frick, ____ child of 76
    Anna Barbara 68
    Christian 79
    Elias 70
    Jacob, dau of 71
    John, child of 75
    Thomas, daus of 56
    Rosena 65
Fulk, John child of 31
Fullmer, Elijah 50
    John dau of 32
Fulmer, Aberhart 69
    David 34

Fulmer, Mrs. George 75
    John 31
    John Frederick 64
    John George 41
    Joseph 50
    Juliann 64
    Mrs. 54
Fulmore, Samuel 76

Gable, Caroline 77
    Caty 3
    Christina 18
    Elisabeth 51
    Eve 13
    Fed 71
    John, children 78
    Joseph 38
    Martha 62
    Mary 71
    Mr. 30
    Nancy 34
    Sarah 64, 76
    Susanna 39
Galle, Mr. 29
Galman, ____ child of 27
Gaminer, Lemuel 58
    Napolian 64
    ____ 17
Gant, Elliot 77
    Dr. Jacob K. 51
Gartman, Abigal 12
    Anna 22
    Anna Margaret 70
    Catharine 76
    Daniel 11
    George 14
    Mrs. 69
    Robert 80
    Susan 8
    Wilm. 15
Geiger, Andrew, son of 66
    Christena 34
    Emanuel, child of 25
    Godfrey 35
    Jacob 37
    John 74
    Mrs. 29
George, Andrew, child of 70
    Joel 55
    Lewis 48, 60
Gibson(?), Caty 44
Gradick, Mrs. 21
Gramner, Jacob 3
Green, ____ child of 52
Gregory, Baruch 32
Griffith, David 60
Grigoery, John 15
Groaner, Nicholas Washington 51
Gross, George, child of 5
    Reuben, child of 51
Grubbs, Enoch 64

Halman, Mary Marthaan 80
    Mrs. 63
    Noah 67
    Noah, child of 37
    Samuel 19
Haltawanger, Adam 58
    David, child of
    Elisabeth 5
    Henry 52
    Mrs. 14
    Rev. 25, 26(2)
Ham, Ellen 81
Hamiter, David 7, 14
    Fannie 7
    Harriet 4
Hanes, Rev. 30
Hare, Edward 71
Harman, ___ 31
    Barbara 10
    Drury J. 45
    Elizabeth 23
    George 14, 27
    Jacob, child of 7, 16
    Joel W. 79
    Julia 51 Mrs. 21
    Rebecca 27
Harmon, Fed, child of 24
    Jacob 1, 3
    Reuben 9
Harris, ___ 60
    Dr. 5
    Mr. 48
    Robert (?), dau of 37
Hart, Henry 8
Hazelius, Dr. 30, 35
Hellebran, Jacob 77
Hendrix, Catharine 21
    Christena 8
    Henry, child of 4, 79
        dau of 57
    John, child of 23
    Lusinda 57
Herman, Nathaniel, child of 76
Hersher, Brother 9(3)
    Rev. 9, 10
Heyler, G., child of 30
High, Henry 10
    John 10
Hillard, Henry 46
Hilliard, ___ Senr., child of 48
Hindrex, Richard 77
Hip, Adam, dau og 73
    Ann 39
    Christena 31
Hipp, John 69
Hix, ___ child of 19
    ___ child of 29
Hohheimer, Mrs. 37
Hoke, Anna 22
    William 23
Hokeheimer, Mrs. 38
Hollow Creek Church 5, 9(2), 13

Holman, David 47
    Samuel 62
    William 33
Holmon, Jacob Senr 53
Holtawanger, George Junr 56
Hook, Albert 58
    Elizabeth 38, 60
    Jefferson, child of 79
    Martin 38
    Rachel 35
    ___ child of 55
Hope, Rev. John C. 25, 28(2), 30
Hornsby, Leah Carline 8
Houck(?), Rev. 23
Houk, Rev. 11, 36(2)
Hoyler, Barnet 13
    Gabriel 12
    Gabriel, child of 25
    Mrs. Gabriel 8
    Polly 16
Huffamer, Jacob, child of 16
Huffman, Capt., child of 17
    Jacob 74
    Jesse 33
    Mary Ann 47
    Miley 22
    Mrs. 15
    Samuel 28
    Mrs. Samuel 27
    Selena 37
Hull, Rev. Mr. 58(3)

Inginer, John 51
Irby, Dr. 11

Jackson, Absalom 60
    Emily 74
    Hirem 58
    Jacob, child of 13
    Mrs. 52(2)
Joe 61(2)
John 61
June 61
Jumper, James 41

Kaigler, Nancy 35
Keasler, Hirem 63
Keisler, Barbara Caroline 63
    Elinder 70
    George 76
Keley, David Milder 3
    Fed., child of 3
Kelly, Adaline 44
    George 44
    Mrs. George 72(2)
    Jacob, child of 17
    Rebecca 26
Kerich, Samuel 10, 55
Kerick, Mrs. 11
Kersh, Gdofrey 1
Kesler, Henry 62

Killian, ___ child of 57
    Eli 52
Kinard, Henry 61
    Michael 29
King, ___ dau. of 74
Kinsler, Jacob, child of 81
    John, dau. of 54
Kleckley, Catharine 21
    Daniel, child of 29
        dau of 65
    Mrs. Daniel 75
    David 29
    Frances 72
    Harriet 7
    Jacob 47
    Mrs. Jacob 6
Kleckly, ___ 36
    Caty 12
    Daniel 26
    David 29
    Henry 37, 67
    Henry, child of 73
    Jacob 7, 22, 57
    Mary 47
    Mary Ann 53
    Mrs. 34
    Nathaniel 37
    Sally 22
Kook, Daniel 70
    Jacob, child of 76
Koon, Christena 36
    Daniel 38
    Mrs. Daniel 42
    David 44
    David, son of 57, 71
    Dr., child of 58
        dau of 61
    Dr. G. 77
    Frank 71(2)
    Mrs. Frank 61
    George Adam 31
    Mrs. George A. 27
    George Michael 36
    Henry 19, 55, 79
    John 67
    Levina 79
    Polly 3
    Mrs. 38
    Mrs., grandson of 38
    Sally 58
    Samuel 2
Kunkle, David child of 66
Kynard, Jacob, dau of 54
Kyzer, David 21

Leaphart, Mrs. George 76
    Mary Ann 64
    Mrs. Michael 16
    Sarah 41
Leaver, William, son of 77
Lee, Col. 6(2)
Lephart, Mariah 70

Lever, Samuel 81
Lewe(?), Elijeana 79
Lewey, John 64
    Ruhem(?) 59
Lewis, John 73
Lexington Court House 24(2), 25, 27(2), 29
Librand/Lybrand church 1(4), 2(2), 3, 4
Like, George, dau of 16
Likes, Mrs. George 74
Lindler, Anna 70
    David, child of 57
    George 42
    Jacob 70
    Jacob, son of 64
    John George 56
    Mary 67
    Michael 49
    Mrs. Michael 57
    Michael, child of 58
    Mrs. 34
    William 58
Lindsey, M. 74
Lips, John 6
Lites, Mrs. Jacob 4
Loid 61
Lominick, Daniel 37, 81
    Susanna 67
Loner, Mr. 48
    Mrs. 74
Long, Christian 21(2)
    Elisabeth 64
    Jacob 68
    John 77
    John Jacob 69
    Mrs. 34
    Polly, son of 55
Long's Church 6, 13(3), 14(3), 24, 25, 27, 28, 29, 36, 37(2), 38(2)
Loreman, Daniel, child of 18
    John, son of 25
    Sally 39
Lorick, Elizabeth Easter 35
    George, child of 4
    Harriet 29
    Capt. Jacob 72
    John 47
    John, dau of 51
    Nancy 46
    Samuel 35
    Wade Alexander 50
Lorman, Jemima 54
Lourick, George 50
Lower Hollow creek Church 47, 48, 50
Lybrand, Ann 58
    Christena 45
    Harriet 20
    Leah 36
    Luesia 70

Lybrand, Lusinda 70
    Martin 69
    Mrs. 39
    Rebecca 69
    Reuben, child of 40
    William, dau of 56
Lykes, George 24
    Jesse 36

McCan, Harriet 80
McCarty, David, child of 79
    Jesse 15
    Joshua 70
McGill, ___ child of 23
McNure, Mrs. 25
    ___ 23

Mabus, William, son of 69
Malur, William, child of 46
Mapier, ___, son of 40
Martin, John 78
Mathias, Christena 27
    John 30, 35
    Mrs. John 33
    John, child of 18
    Mary, Luesia 61
    Mrs. 16
    Rachel 33
    Thomas 62
Mayer, Adam 31
    Anna Catherine 57
    George 75
    Jacob 31, 54(2), 55(2),
        56(4), 57(4)
    Jacob, son of 47, 62
    Mary Magdalen 49
    Mrs. 6
    Uriah 60, 61
    Mrs. Ulrick 55
Mayes, Mrs. George 74
Mealy, Rev. Mr. 10, 20
Meetze, Father 17(4), 18(2), 19,
    20(2), 21(3), 28
    Mrs. 45
Meetze's church--see St. Peter's
Melton, Mrs. 74
Merryman, Mrs. 61
Metz, Adam 75
    Barbara Ann 79
    Daniel 33
    Mrs. Daniel 32, 80
    Daniel, child of 28
        grandchild of 80
        son of 61
    George 75
    Henry 31, 47
    Henry, child of 11
    Jacob Albert 47
    John, child of 5
    Mary 13
    Mrs. 28, 46
    Naomi 19

Metz, Peter 41
    Sally 62
    Samuel 13
    Sparta 41
    Thomas 41
Metze, Brother 2, 3, 4, 5(2), 7
    Catharine 12
    David 9
    Father 10, 11, 12(3),
        14(2), 15(2), 17
    Mrs. Jacob 14
    Mr. 5
    Rebeckah 10
    Rev. 8, 9(4), 10(2)
Miller, Rev. Adam 39, 61(2)
    Capt., child of 34
        son of 30
    David 39
    David, child of 54
        son of 56
    Father 9
    Capt. Geroge 35
    Henry 41
    Henry, son of 61
    Mrs. J. 80
    Jeremiah 48
    John 54, 56
    John Adam 53
    Miss 59
    Mrs. 34
    Polly 78
    Rev. Mr. 42
    Widow 44
Miller, children of 34
Minnick, Henry 62
Monts, George 54, 61
    George, son of 74
    John 22
    John, son of 51
    Julian 58
    Nancy 64
    Sally 67
Moser, ___ 10
    Brother 6(2), 24, 31
    Mr. 67, 68(5)
Mought, ___ 12
Mount Calvary Church 27, 29,
    30, 42, 44
Myer, John, dau of 57

Nazareth Church (Sandhills)
    10(3), 12(2), 13,
    15, 16, 17(2), 18(4),
    19(3), 20, 21, 22(2),
    23(3), 24(2), 25,
    26, 27
Nehemyer, Henry 62
Nichols, Anna Catharine 13
    Jacob 2, 3
    Margaret 3

Nichols, Mrs. 3
Nipper, Mary 38
Nunemaker, David 23
    Harriet 32
    Jacob 6
Nunnemaker, Jacob 31
    Lavall, 31

Oswald, Joseph W. 44
Oswalt, David 55
    David, children of 59
    Emanuel 59
    George 60
    George, children of 59
        dau of 59
    Mrs. George 56
    Sally 49
    _____ 66
Owens, Jesse 17
Oxner, John 19
Oxoner, Daniel 53
    Daniel, dau of 70
    Henry 61

Paton, Mr. 66
Peterson, Rev. Mr. 64
Pilgrim's Church (Davidson Co, NC) 34
Piney Woods Church--see St. Peter's
Platt, Abel 67
Poor House 18(2)
Price, Ann Elisabeth(?) 65
    Christian 49, 70
    Daniel, child of 78
    Flora 48
    Harriet 62
    Isaiah 63
    Jacob 72
    John 39, 66
    Joseph 64
    Miley 77
    Mrs. 47
    Rebeca 67
    Sally 72
    Wilm. 70

Rackard, George 5
Rall, Caroline 55
    Charlotte 45
    Christian 64
    Father 24(2)
    John 7
    Mary 67
Rameck, Mrs. Peter 40
Ramick, Mr 65
Rankins church 35
Rauch, ___ 8, 9, 10, 17, 24(2), 28
    Brother 2, 23
    Elizabeth 23
    Julia 20
    Mrs. 24
    Rev. 20, 21
    Rev., dau of 16

Rauch, Tempy 11
Ray, Catharine W. 23
    Harriet 58
Revis, Capt. 2
Rhodes, Mr. 55(5), 56(6)
Rice, Joel, child of 54
Riddle, Mrs. 54
Rieves, Harriet 7
Rinehart, Catharine Elizabeth 24
    Mr. 20
    Miss Mary 69
    Mary 53
Rinehart's church 27
Riseinger, Mrs. 65
    Radama 66
Rish, Wilm. 78
Risinger, David 72
    John 67
    Mr. 57
    Mrs. 73
    Rebecca 64
    _____ dau of 61
Rister, Adam church of 36
    Mrs. 35
    William, child of 57
Roberts, Adam 11
    Adam, child of 29
    George, child of 14, 27
    dau of 38
    Mrs. George, 14, 29
    Noah 26 Molly 1
Rolen, Abigail 50
Roll ,
    Nancy 40
Roof, Barbara 45
    Benjamin 45, 68
    Ben, sister of 44
    Mrs. Benjamin 25
    David 34
    Elizabeth 1
    Jesse 68
    Mrs. John 66
    Lorence 37
    Mrs. 46
    Nancy 15, 54
    Sharlet 38
Rouch, Caty 15
    Luesia 9
Rudisal, Rev. E. 70
Rudisill, Dr. 70
Rudy, Rev. 10
Ryster, Anna Magdalen 45

St. _____ 63
St. Jacob's church 77(3), 78(2), 79(5), 80(4), 81(3)
St. James church 4(2), 5(3), 6(3), 7(4), 8(5), 9(3), 10, 11(3), 12(2), 13, 14

St. John's church 1(3), 2(2),
    6, 7, 10, 12, 22, 25, 26(7),
    27(4), 28(5), 29(3), 30(6),
    31(8), 32(8), 33(8), 34(9),
    35(7), 36(3), 37(3), 38(3),
    39(3), 40(5), 41(4), 42(4),
    43(2), 44(4), 45(2), 46(2),
    47(4), 48(2), 49(3), 50(3),
    51(4), 52(3), 53(3), 54(4),
    55(4), 56(4), 57(2), 58(2),
    59(4), 60(3), 61, 62(5),
    63(4), 64(4), 65(4), 66(3),
    67(4), 68(3), 69(4), 70(2),
    71(4), 72(4), 73(4), 74(3),
    74(3), 75(3), 76(5), 77(3),
    78(2), 79(3), 80(2), 81(2)
St. John's church (Charleston) 19
St. Johns church (near Jacob
    Rawls) 27
St. Johns church (near Leaphart) 29
St. Luke's church 5, 8, 19,
    20(5), 22, 25(3), 27
St. Mark's church 21, 23(2), 24(4),
    25(5), 26(3), 29, 57
St. Mathew's Church 7, 28
St. Matthews church (Amelia) 8,
    16(2)
St. Mathews Church (Orangeburg)
    17, 22, 27
St. Michael's church 1(6), 2(6),
    3(5), 4(4), 5(6), 6(5), 7(5),
    8(5), 9(7), 10(7), 11(6),
    12(4), 13(3), 14(2), 15(5),
    16(5), 17(6), 18(5), 19(7),
    20(6), 21(6), 22(5), 23(2),
    25(3), 26(3), 27(3), 28(5),
    29(4), 30(3)
St. P---- 64, 69
St. Pauls Church (Little Hollow
    Creek) 9, 13, 14, 22, 27, 34,
    36, 37(3), 38(2), 40(3),
    41(3), 42(3), 43(2), 44(4),
    45(2), 46(2), 47, 48, 49,
    50(2), 51(2), 52(5),
    53(3), 54, 55(3), 56(2),
    57(2), 58(3), 59(2),
    60(2), 61(2), 62(3),
    63(4), 64(2), 65(4), 66(2),
    67(3), 68(2), 69(2), 70,
    71(5), 72(4), 73(2), 74(4),
    75(4), 76(4), 77(5), 78(5),
    79(3), 80(6), 81
St. PetersChurch 1(5), 2(5), 3(4),
    4(5), 5(4), 6(4), 7(4), 8(5),
    9(7), 10(5), 11(5), 12(4),
    13(3), 14(4), 15(4), 16(4),
    17(4), 18(5), 19(6), 20(6),
    21(5), 22(3), 23(4), 24(3),
    25, 26(2), 28, 29, 31(2),
    33(3), 34(2), 35(2), 36(2),
    37(5), 38(3), 39(4), 40(5),
    41(5), 42(3), 43(4), 44(5),
    45(3), 46(2), 47(4),
    48(2), 49(2), 50(6),
    51(7), 52(4), 53(5),
    54(4), 55(2), 56(4),
    57(2), 58(4), 59(5),
    60(3), 61(3), 62(7),
    63(5), 64(4), 65(8),
    66(6), 67(3), 68(2),
    69(2), 70(5), 71(6),
    72(9), 73(7), 74(7),
    75(3), 76(9), 77(9),
    78(6), 79(4), 80(6),
    81(6)

St. Peters (Meetze's)
    Church 39, 41, 62,
    67, 68(2), 69,
    75(2)

St. Peters (Piney Woods)
    church 8, 22, 27,
    30(2), 31(2), 32(5),
    33(2), 34(2), 35(5),
    36(3), 37(2), 38(3),
    39(2), 42(3), 43(3),
    44(2), 45(3), 46(3),
    47(2), 48(5), 49, 51,
    52(2), 57, 60, 67(2),
    68(2), 69(2), 70, 76,
    78, 79(4), 80(2)

Salem Church (Hollow Creek)
    11, 13, 14, 35,
    36(2), 37(2), 38(3),
    39(4), 40(5), 41(3),
    42(3), 43(2), 44(4),
    45(3), 46(3), 47(3),
    48(4), 49(4), 50(3),
    51(2), 52(6), 53(4),
    54(2), 55(4), 56(3),
    57(4), 58(3), 59(4),
    60(3), 61(2), 62(3),
    63(4), 64(4), 65(3),
    66(4), 67(3), 68,
    69(4), 70(3), 71(5),
    72(2), 73(4), 74(3),
    75(4), 76(4), 77(5),
    78(4), 79(5), 80(5),
    81(2)
Salem Church(Little Saluda)
    13
Salser, Ezekiel 14
Sandy Run Church 1(2), 2,
    3, 4, 7, 11, 14, 15,
    17, 24, 25
Sarah, child of 65
Scheck _____ 35
Scheek, _____ 24
Schick, Brother 24
    Brother, child of
        24
    dau of 24

Schoolhouse (Below Cloud's
    Creek) 13
    (Near Stephen Bowers)
    66
Schwartz, Adam, child of 60
    Rev. John 17, 24(3)
Scott, Edwin, child of 24
    Richard 35
    _____ 10
    _____ child of 18
Sea, Billy, child of 80
    Jefferson 77
    Mountain, son of 77
Sease, Anna 47
    Elias 79
    Elisabeth 65
    Fed 51
    Fed, mother-in-law of 51
    Henry 56
    John Leonard 65
    Mary Caroline 49
    Mrs. 45
    _____ 31
Seastrunk, Emanuel 53
    Emmanuel 41
    Harriet 74
    Henry 29
    Mary Magdalene 5
See, Maintam (?) 57
    Miss 14
    Widow 56
    William 2, 66
Senn, Conrad 36
    Epsy 70
    Jacob(?) 48
    Sally 70
    Widow 32
Settsler, John 62
    Mary 57
Setzler, Elisabeth 72
    John 65
    Martin 77
Sharp, Francis 70
    Martha Ann Elisabeth 62
Shealey, Mary 41
Shealy, Adam 56, 65, 66(4),
    67(2), 68, 69(2), 70,
    71(2), 72, 72(3), 74(2),
    80
    Mrs. Adam 75
    Andrew 49
    Daniel 65, 70
    Elisabeth 59
    Elisabeth Harriet 77
    Emanuel 67
    Henry 53, 55
    Jesse 52
    John George 44
    Josiah 56
    Levi, child of 65
        mother in law of
            65

Shealy, Mr. 65
    Samuel, dau of 70
    Solomon 77
    Wiley 80
    William 67
    William, child of 79
    Mrs. William 71
Shearer, Brother 2(2), 3
Sheley, Levi 41
Sherlock, Mary 19
Shoneback, Rev. 9
Shular, Conrod 3
    Rebekah 1
    _____ child of 2
Shuler, Elizabeth 14
    Mrs. John 16
    Mrs. 12
Shull, Adam 20
    Adam, child of 46
        son of 69
    Caroline 67
    Charlotte 45
    David 54
    Margaret 68
    William 38
    William, dau of 67, 72
Shwartz, Henry 76
Sikes, Mary Ann 68
Sinah 61
Sites, Christian 63
Slice, George, son of 57, 69
    Jacob, child of 48
    John George 38
    Mathias, child of 52
    Mr. 37
Sligh, Benjamin 58
    Mary Magdalen 59
    Nicholas, son of 32
    Thomas, son of 31
Slight, Mrs. Nicholas 37
Slise, George, child of 43
    Jacob 45
Slone, Clarisa 68
    Samuel 73
    Winford E. 37
    _____ 62
Smith, James 4
    Jemima 6
    S. H. 35
Smoke--see also Rauch, Rouch
    Brother 2, 4, 16(2), 18
    Mrs. 4
Snyder, Catharine 46
Son, Jacob David 80
Souter, Dr. 34
Sox, Margaret Catharine 61
    Godleab 50
    Jacob 39
    Jesse 62
    Martin 36
    Martin, son of 76
    Mary 67

Srums(?), ___ child of 8
Spring Hill 29
S. S. 61
Stack, Abraham 19
    Catherine 60
    Godfrey, son of 50
    Jacob 13
    John 12, 19
    Lewis 76
    Lewis, child of 12, 15, 17
        dau of 50, 76
    Martha 41, 72
    Mary 49
Stack, ___ child of 17
Stewert, Alexander 6
Stingley, Barbara 3
    Mrs. George 4
    John 7
Stingly, Jacob 8
Stone, James 60
    Mrs. James 63
    Mrs. 33
    William 53
Stoney Battery--see St. Luke's
Stoutemyer, John, son of 75
Stoutmier, Eve Margaret 42
Stoutmyer, Magdalen, dau of 56
Stroble, Rev. 21, 22, 23
Stuck, Mr., grandson of 58
    Mrs. 42
Suber, Nancy 30
Sultan, Caroline 79
    John, child of 48
    Mrs. John H. 50
Sulton, John 71
    Joseph 64
    Julian 35
    Robert, child of 81
    _____ 68
Summer, Andrew, child of 27
        dau of 44
    George 32
    John Frances 79
    John N. 30
    Harriet 30
    Michael 60
    William 31
Summers, Mrs. 49
Sweetenberg, William 30
Swigard, Christian 54
    Christian, son of 51
    Elisa 64
    Jacob 23
    Major, child of 64
    Samuel 16
    Sanders 29
    Sanders, son of 50
Swittenberg, Easter 50

Tarrer, Andrew 51
    Christinah 9
    Harriet 51
    Henry 3

Tarrer, Jessee 22, 51
    John Jacob 51
    Malinda 33
    Susanna 30
Tayler, David, child of 57
    Elias, son of 64
    Mrs. Elias 74
    Joel 70
    Joshua 39
    Mrs. 60
Taylor, Mrs. 30
    William 1
Thompson, John 13
Todd, ___ child of, 26
Trapp, Laban H. 67
Turnipseed, Elisa 22
    Jacob 19
    Mary 41

Vansant, John 68
    Mrs. 77
    Reubin, child of 62
Veal, Ann E. 77
Veale, Thomas L. 7
Viel, Prisilla 51
Vinsant, Nancy 48
    Nicholas 53
    Reuben 48

Waddle, Mary Ann 52
Waite, Allen, child of 26
Warner, Thomas, child of 53
Warren, Mrs. 57
Wateree Creek Church--see St.
    Jacob's Church
Wead, Mrs., child of 14
Weed, Anna 15
    Barbara 35
    Christian, child of 28,
        42(2)
    Elizabeth 2, 29
    John 13
    John, child of 13
    Joseph 41
    Milly 68
    Presilla 33
    Rebecca 13
    Sousen, child of 35
Wessels, The Rev. 14(2)
Wessinger, Amey 34
    Caroline 57
    Christian 8
    George 73
    George, son of 67
    Henry 70
    Jesse 58
    John 54
    Mary Ann 65
    Mary Magdalen 39
    Mathias 8
    Uriah 54, 69
    Uriah George 68

Wheeler, Capt., child of 61
    Elisabeth 64
    George 45
    Jacob 31
    Levi 74
    Mary Ann 64
    Mr. 33
    Mrs. 60
    Simion 48
    Simon, child of 54
White, George 12
    John (Whites?) 41
    Mrs. John 69
Whites, Elisabeth 76
    William 64
Wick, Pamelia 44
Wicker, John 62
Wiggar, Gerard, child of 46
Wigger, ____ 8
Williams, Mrs. 78
Williamson, Mr. Nathan 66
Wilson, David 36
    Mrs. David 72
    John 74
    William 43
Wingard, Adam 31
    Catharine 19
    Christian 13
    Daniel 38
    Daniel, son of 49
    Elijah 77
    Elizabeth 23
    Gabriel 69
    George 24, 39, 58
    Henry 79
    Jacob 23
    Jeremiah 48
    John 12, 13, 47
    John, son of 21
    Joshua, child of 23
        son of 39
    Milly 11
    Mrs. 64
    Nancy 39
    Reuben, son of 61
    Rubin(?), son of 59
    Samuel 67
    Mrs. Samuel 40
    Thomas A. 64
    William 2
    ____ 17(4), 18, 19, 20
Wise, Capt. 31
    Elizabeth 1, 4
    Fed, child of 27
    George 1
    George, child of 4
    John 6, 7, 8(2), 24, 34
    Mrs. John 22
    Kiza 26
    Mary Cat 31
    Widow 4

Younginer, Adam 76
    Daniel 57
    David 55
    David, child of 40(2)
    Mary 30
    Mrs., son of 50
    Sebastian 50
    Sharlet 6
    Susanna 80
    Susannah 10

Zion Church 6(3), 7, 8, 9(4),
10(3), 11(3), **12**(5), 13(3),
14(3), 15(7), 16(6), 18(6),
19(6), 20(7), 21(8),
22(5), 23(6), 24(3),
25(4), 26(4), 27(4),
28(7), 29(4), 30(4),
31(5), 32(3), 33(5),
34(5), 35(6), 37(5),
38(3), 39(4), 40(4),
41(3), 42(4), 43(3),
44(3), 45(2), 46(3),
47(4), 48(2), 49(3),
50(3), 51(4), 52(3),
53(5), 54(3), 55(5),
56(5), 57(3), 58(3),
59(4), 60(3), 61(2),
62(2), 63(5), 64(3),
65(3), 66(4), 67(5),
68(3), 69(2), 70(6),
71(6), 72(4), 73(5),
74(6), 75(4), 76(7),
78(5), 79(4), 80(4),
81(3)

Index prepared by Miss Karon Mac Smith, Nixon, Texas

www.ingramcontent.com/pod-product-compliance
Lightning Source LLC
Chambersburg PA
CBHW031426290426
44110CB00011B/544